Advanced Painting & Decorating

Page 178

NOTICE TO READERS

For safety, use caution, care and good judgment when following the procedures described in this book. The Publisher and Black & Decker cannot assume responsibility for any damage to property or injury to persons as a result of misuse of the information provided.

The techniques shown in this book are general techniques for various applications. In some instances, additional techniques not shown in this book may be required.

Always follow manufacturers' instructions included with products, since deviating from the directions may void warranties. The projects in this book vary widely as to skill levels required: some may not be appropriate for all do-it-yourselfers, and some may require professional help.

Consult your local Building Department for information on building permits, codes and other laws as they apply to your project.

THE COMPLETE GUIDE TO PAINTING & DECORATING
Created by: The Editors of Creative Publishing international, Inc., in cooperation with Black & Decker. Black & Decker is a trademark of The Black & Decker Corporation and is used under license.

Library of Congress Cataloging-in-Publication Data
The complete guide to painting & decorating.
  p.   cm.
  --At head of title: Black & Decker.
  ISBN 1-58923-262-3 (softcover)
  1. House painting. 2. Interior decoration. 3. Paperhanging.
I. Black & Decker Corporation (Towson, Md.) II. Creative Publishing International. III. Title: Complete guide to painting and decorating. IV. Title: Black & Decker. V. Title: Black & Decker the complete guide to painting & decorating.
TT323.C66 1999
698'. 14--dc21
                                      99-23622

Portions of *The Complete Guide to Painting & Decorating* were previously published in *Decorating With Paint & Wallcovering.*

Other books offered from this publisher include:
Complete Guide to Home Wiring, Complete Guide to Home Plumbing, Complete Guide to Building Decks, Complete Guide to Home Masonry, Complete Guide to Creative Landscapes, Complete Guide to Home Carpentry, Complete Guide to Home Storage, Complete Guide to Windows & Doors, Complete Guide to Bathrooms, Complete Guide to Easy Woodworking Projects, Complete Guide to Ceramic & Stone Tile, Complete Guide to Flooring, Complete Guide to Roofing & Siding, Complete Guide to Ceramic & Stone Tile, Complete Guide to Kitchens, Complete Guide to Outdoor Wood Projects, Complete Photo Guide to Home Repair, Complete Photo Guide to Home Improvement, Complete Photo Guide to Outdoor Home Improvement

BLACK & DECKER®

THE COMPLETE GUIDE TO

PAINTING &
DECORATING

...allpaper in Home Decor

Creative Publishing
international

CHANHASSEN, MINNESOTA
www.creativepub.com

I2105752

Contents

Creative Publishing international

Copyright© 2006
Creative Publishing international, Inc.
18705 Lake Drive East
Chanhassen, Minnesota 55317
1-800-328-3895
www.creativepub.com
All rights reserved
Printed by: R.R. Donnelley
10 9 8 7 6 5 4 3 2 1

President/CEO: Ken Fund
Vice President/Sales & Marketing:
Kevin Haas

For Revised Edition:
Executive Editor: Bryan Trandem
Editors: Jerri Farris, Tom Lemmer
Assistant Managing Editor: Tracy Stanley
Photo Director: Tim Himsel
Art Director: Dave Schelitzche
Page Layout: Kari Johnston
Photo Acquisition Editor: Julie Caruso
Lead Photographer: Steve Galvin
Photographers: Andrea Rugg, Joel Schnell
Scene Shop Carpenter: Randy Austin
Production Manager: Linda Halls

THE COMPLETE GUIDE TO PAINTING &
DECORATING
ISBN 10: 1-58923-262-3
ISBN 13: 978-1-58923-262-4

Introduction

*I*n a recent year, Americans spent an astounding quarter of a trillion dollars to remodel and redecorate their homes. Of that amount, more than $7 million were spent on paint and wallcoverings. According to the National Realtor's Association, painting is the most popular do-it-yourself project of them all. One reason is that almost everyone believes they can slap paint or paper on a wall. And while that's true, it takes much more than that to create a truly professional-looking decorating job.

The Complete Guide to Painting & Decorating contains all the information you need to approach any painting or decorating project like a pro. It's filled with color photographs and concise do-it-yourself instructions that lead you through everything from painting walls, ceilings, floors and furniture to hanging wallpaper on walls and ceilings. The book is divided into four easy-to-follow sections: Color & Decorating Principles, Basic Painting & Wallcovering, Advanced Painting & Decorating, and Painting Furniture.

Beginning with Color & Decorating Principles, you will learn about color theory and how to choose color schemes that suit your room, as well as your personal tastes. This section explains in detail the effects of colors, the different types of color schemes, and the varieties of patterns. Within its pages, you'll discover how to use color and pattern to create a mood in a room and how to finalize a room design.

The next section, Basic Painting & Wallcovering, illustrates the methods professionals use to paint walls and ceilings, stain woodwork, and hang wallcoverings on walls and ceilings. The basic painting section starts with an introduction to the vital steps of preparation, continues with information on choosing paint and equipment, and then walks you through the process of applying paint and cleaning up after the project. The section on staining shows you how to achieve smooth, even finishes on woodwork. The material on wallcovering techniques covers the processes of choosing wallcoverings, estimating quantities, and selecting tools and materials, as well as preparing and hanging wallcoverings.

The Advanced Painting & Decorating section demonstrates how to embellish walls and floors with faux finishes and decorative accents. Fads are especially common in decorative painting, which has led to an explosion of tools and equipment claiming to provide perfect finishes with little to no experience or effort. Like anything else that sounds too good to be true, some of these products are disappointments waiting to happen. Others are easy-to-use, effective tools that make it easier and more fun than ever to produce fascinating faux finishes. This section introduces you to a range of tools, materials, and finishes that are within the abilities and budgets of most do-it-yourselfers.

The final section, Painting Furniture, leads you through a range of projects that produce interesting, unique finishes on wood furnishings for your home. Here you'll learn to produce smooth finishes and interesting effects on furnishings of all sorts.

Color & Decorating Principles

Understanding Color

*A*lthough some people know instinctively how to choose effective color combinations, the majority of us need to rely on color theory to select colors that enhance our homes.

Basic color theory is illustrated with a color wheel. The color wheel shows how colors, also called *hues,* are related. The colors on the color wheel are classified as either primary or secondary. Combinations of these colors are described as either related or complementary, based on their position on the color wheel.

Red, yellow, and blue are primary colors. Orange, green, and purple are secondary colors, made by combining two primary colors. All paint colors are created from some combination of white, black, and primary colors.

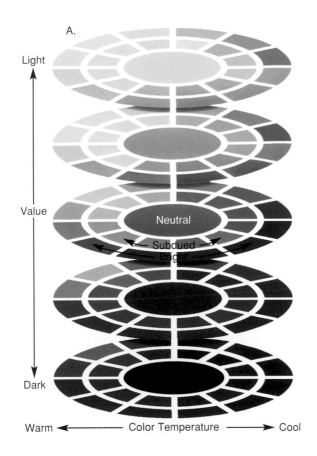

Light

Value

Neutral

Subdued

Bright

Dark

Warm ← Color Temperature → Cool

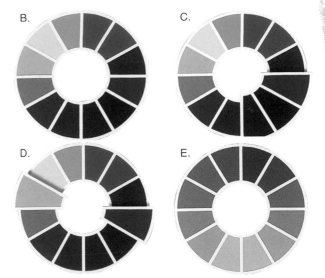

A: The dimensions of color are illustrated with these variations of the color wheel. Colors range in value, brightness, and temperature. All colors are made from some combination of white, black, and primary colors. B: The color wheel illustrates how the basic colors are related. C: Related colors are those next to one another on the color wheel. D: Complementary colors are located opposite one another on the color wheel. E: Neutral colors are shades of white, gray, or beige.

Related colors are those next to one another on the color wheel. For example, red and orange are related colors.

Complementary colors are located opposite each other on the color wheel. Blue, for example, is the complement of orange.

Neutral colors are shades of white, gray, or beige. Most neutrals are tinted slightly with another color.

Colors are also classified by their value, saturation, and temperature. In this section, you will learn about how each of these properties affects the way we respond to colors.

The *value* of a hue is determined by the amount of white or black present and is expressed in terms of a color's lightness or darkness. Light colors have a greater percentage of white; dark colors contain more black.

Saturation describes the brightness of a hue. Saturated hues, also called bright colors, are intense hues that are undiluted by black, white, or a complementary color. Desaturated colors, also called subdued colors, are formed when a hue is diluted with white, black, or a complementary hue.

Colors are also described as being either *warm* or *cool*. Warm hues are variations of red, orange, yellow, and brown; cool hues are variations of green, blue, and purple.

CREAM (W)   (W)

T-65   T-117   (W)   G SEA (W)   T-122   T-140

Light Colors

ight colors help create bright, spacious-feeling rooms. To the eye, light colors seem to recede, making rooms appear larger and ceilings higher. Since light colors reflect light well, they can brighten a north-facing room, a closet, or a dark hallway.

Whites and other light colors are good choices for a nursery or a child's bedroom. In any room, white walls form a neutral background that does not compete with furnishings.

Wall roughness and paint sheen can affect the lightness of any color. Smooth surfaces and gloss paints reflect maximum light to make a color seem lighter. Rough-textured walls and flat-sheen paints hold more shadow and minimize the lightness of a color.

8 TH 9 GINGER PINK (W)   T-28   T-65   T-117   (W)   G SEA (W)   T-122

8 TH 10 CICELY (M)   E (W)   CK (W)   ESS SEA (M)

8 TH 12 M   EEY

S-25

Dark Colors

Use dark colors to create an intimate room. Because dark colors absorb light, walls appear closer and make the room seem smaller. Dark colors are most often used in libraries, studies, and other quiet areas.

Dark colors can be used to disguise problem areas, such as uneven walls, or to make a high ceiling seem lower. In heavy-use areas, dark colors can hide wear. Rough surfaces and flat-paint finishes make colors seem darker because they absorb more light.

Dark walls tend to dominate, so you may want to use lighter-colored accents to add balance to a dark room.

50 TH 20 GOLDEN YE

50 TH 21 LIBERT

50 TH 22 NA

50 TH 2

50 TH 7 CARMINE (R)

50 TH 8 CINDER RED

50 TH 9 SIRO

50 TH

50 TH 14 ORANGE FLIP (O)

50 TH 15 JUICY FRUIT (O)

50 TH 16 EARTH TILE (U)

50 TH 17 BRIGHT ORANGE (O)

Warm Colors

Reds, yellows, browns, oranges, and peaches are warm colors. Intense warm colors create exciting spaces, while subdued warm colors form pleasant rooms for social gatherings. Warm colors are often used in eating areas, like breakfast or dining rooms.

Warm colors also help make north-facing rooms more inviting. Research has shown that people actually feel warmer in a room painted with yellows, reds, or oranges than they do in a white or blue room. In colder climates, warm colors are a popular choice.

22 TH 2 OVERSEA

BLOSSO

22 TH 3 BOUT

VELY LIL

22 TH 4

H 4 LILA

22 TH

29 TH

28 TH 2 BLUE DRIFT (W)

28 TH 3 SCANDINAVIA (W)

28 TH 4 BRIGHT EYES (M)

28 TH 5 VAGRANT BLUE (M)

28 TH 6 DEEP NIGHT (D)

L-123

Cool Colors

*B*lues, greens, lavenders, and grays are cool colors. Intense cool colors are fresh and dramatic, while subdued cool grays are tranquil. Cool colors make rooms feel less confining. They are often used in bathrooms and other small rooms, as well as in bedrooms and formal living areas.

Use cool colors in west-facing kitchens, porches, and other areas where afternoon heat is a problem. In very warm climates, using whites and cool colors exclusively can make an entire house seem more comfortable.

S-123

L-1

27 TH 13

T-12

50

27 TH 15 CATALINA (W)

T-133

27 TH 16 ROBE BLUE (M)

(W)

27 TH 17 LIMPID

27 TH 18 BLUE

S-123

S-131

L-130

L-36

15 TH 6 LUSTY YELLOW (D)

05-

Bright Colors

Bright colors are highly saturated with pigment. They are created by pure hues that are not diluted by white or darkened by black. Bright colors command attention and work well in active spaces, such as recreation rooms, sun porches, and children's rooms. In rooms that receive little natural light, such as a basement recreation room, painting the walls a bright color will help the room seem less dreary.

Because bright colors draw attention, they are often used as bold accents in rooms with a neutral or subdued color scheme. Balancing a single dominant bright color with neutral furnishings and elements creates another effective color scheme. Bright colors create a sense of excitement and energy and should be used with restraint in rooms intended for relaxing.

Subdued Colors

Subdued colors are less saturated with pigment than bright colors. These desaturated colors are created by adding a mixture of white, black, or gray to a pure hue. The greater the percentage of these added colors, the more neutral the base color becomes. Subdued colors are relaxing and restful and are frequently used to create a tranquil mood in bedrooms, studies, and other quiet retreats. The quiet nature of subdued colors also makes them a popular choice for bathrooms and dressing rooms.

Subdued colors should be carefully balanced with neutral- or bright-colored features. Add interest to a room with a dominant subdued color by featuring a few brightly colored accents.

Building a Color Scheme

*A*new color scheme can dramatically change a room or your entire home. Even without changes of furniture or carpeting, a fresh infusion of color and pattern can transform the most ordinary room into an inviting living space.

Most room designs use one of three basic color schemes. A *single-color scheme,* also called a monochromatic scheme, uses one color in varying shades, such as light and dark blues. A *related color scheme,* sometimes called an analogous scheme, features two or three colors that are next to each other on the color wheel. A room decorated in blues and lavenders is an example of a related color scheme. A *complementary color scheme* uses colors that are opposite each other on the color wheel, like peach and blue.

Since color schemes are based on very personal choices, your rooms should feature color combinations you enjoy. But knowing exactly which colors to choose can be difficult. The following pages will help you select color schemes that suit your needs and tastes. In the following pages, you will discover how the color scheme affects the appearance of a room and the way it makes you feel. Knowing the effects of individual colors, which you learned in the last section, you will be able to apply the information in this section to combine colors in a way that serves the needs of a particular room.

Single-color Scheme

A single-color scheme uses varying shades of the same color. Single-color schemes are easy to develop and lend a restful feeling to a room. These schemes offer much more variety than you might expect.

Varying the color values—including both light and dark values—and featuring some neutral-toned elements help keep a room interesting and balanced. The intensity of the colors you choose and the types of pattern work together to create effects that range from quietly subtle to outrageously dramatic. In addition to building a scheme around a pure color, you can use white or a neutral color, such as beige or gray, as the basis for a single-color scheme.

In general, the lighter elements in a single-color scheme tend to stand out the most. Highlight the most attractive features of the room with light colors, and use dark colors to downplay the less attractive features. In small homes, repeating a single color scheme with a variety of patterns and textures in adjoining rooms helps tie the rooms together.

Related Color Scheme

Using varying shades of two or three colors located close together on the color wheel creates a related color scheme. For instance, a selection of blue, purple, and violet hues forms a harmonious related scheme, as does a combination of various yellows and greens. The values of the colors you feature will determine the overall feeling of the room. Related light colors will have a relaxing effect, while related dark colors will make the room seem more elegant and formal.

A room decorated with a related scheme has a unified, quiet feeling. Although this is a relatively easy scheme to create, the colors should be carefully balanced to avoid giving the room a one-dimensional appearance. To avoid creating a flat room, choose one or two dominant colors. Then, add accents to these colors, using hues that are farther away on the color wheel from the dominant colors. For example, if you are working with a lavender and blue related scheme, feature various shades of lavender and pale blue for some of the room's most dominant features, and select a few dark blue and purple accents. To give the scheme balance, use neutral shades, such as white, cream, or gray, in other dominant features.

Complementary Color Scheme

Complementary color schemes range from cheerful and vibrant to arresting and dramatic. These schemes are formed by using variations of colors located opposite one another on the color wheel, such as peach and pale blue, or pink and light green. In a successful complementary scheme, the colors play off each other to bring out the best in the contrasting hues. A simple way to work with a complementary scheme is to choose one group of warm colors and another group of contrastingly cool colors. Complementary colors can be equally balanced, or one color can dominate the scheme to give the room an overall warm or cool tone.

As with a related color scheme, the hues comprising a complementary scheme must be carefully balanced and include some neutral-toned elements to soften the contrast in the complementary tones. Decide whether you want the room to have an overall light or dark tone, then choose accent colors opposite in tone. For example, a light complementary scheme is created by selecting pale complementary colors and light-colored neutrals for the dominant features and darker complementary accents.

Using Pattern

*P*atterns increase visual interest and texture in a decorating scheme. Although wallcoverings and upholstered furniture are the boldest ways to introduce pattern to a room, subtler pattern accents, such as window treatments, area rugs, and small throw pillows are also effective. A well-designed room may use only one pattern or many different patterns that are related by color or style.

The following pages illustrate how all patterns can be classified in one of four categories: geometric patterns, large patterns, small patterns, and overall patterns. Each pattern type can greatly influence a room's style. For example, a bold, abstract print wallcovering immediately establishes a contemporary style, while a wallcovering with a small floral design will suggest a more traditional or country theme.

Pattern works hand-in-hand with color scheme. As you read this section, pay attention to the ways in which the colors in a patterned wallcovering, carpet, or window treatment can enhance the overall color scheme of a room.

Like colors, patterns have an effect on the way you perceive a room. In this section, you'll see how patterns can create an illusion of height or space. You'll also learn about how the type of pattern affects a room's tone. Having an awareness of the visual effects and characteristics of each pattern type will help you achieve the look you want.

Geometric Patterns

*P*laids, stripes, grids, and checks are some of the most common geometric patterns featured in decorating schemes. Large geometric patterns tend to be bold and exciting; when used as a dominant feature they have a stimulating effect. However, if used sparingly they add a touch of surprise and charm. Small geometric patterns leave a more subtle impression, quietly introducing accent colors into a room's color scheme. To prevent a room from looking too busy, balance dominant geometric patterns with solid-color accents.

Unlike other patterns, geometric patterns can emphasize a room's architectural attributes or downplay its flaws. When skillfully applied, a geometric pattern can create optical illusions. For instance, patterns with strong vertical lines can make a ceiling seem higher, and patterns with strong horizontal lines can help tall features appear shorter.

Large Patterns

Florals, fruits, and vegetables are just a few of the designs commonly found on wallcoverings and fabrics with large patterns. In general, large patterns are stimulating and look best in an active area, such as a child's room, large kitchen, hallway, playroom, or family room. Use large patterns sparingly in rooms typically used for relaxing, such as bedrooms and master bathrooms. When carefully chosen, a few large-patterned accents—such as an area rug, throw pillow, or small-scale window treatment—will add a spark of interest to a room's overall color scheme. In most cases, it's best to feature only one large pattern in a room. If there is more than one, the patterns lose their charm and the room looks too busy.

Like dark colors, large patterns seem to advance toward you, making rooms feel smaller and more cozy. A large-patterned wallcovering is a sure way to make a large, intimidating room feel more inviting. Large patterns may be included in the decorating scheme for a small room, but if they are featured too prominently, the room will feel crowded.

Small Patterns

Small patterns add a touch of contrast to the background color scheme, quietly enhancing its effect. Like light colors, small patterns appear to recede, making close spaces seem larger and more open. For this reason, they are often used to create an illusion of space in small kitchens and bathrooms.

Small patterns have a tendency to "wash out," or lose their visual impact, when used over large wall or floor spaces. If you would like to use a small-patterned wallcovering or carpeting, balance the print with solids or with another pattern style. On walls, for instance, a coordinating large-patterned border can be used at crown molding or chair rail height to break up a small pattern. Similarly, a small area rug with a large or overall pattern can be used to balance small-print carpeting. It is often difficult to imagine how a small pattern will look when used over a large area, so try to get as large a sample as possible to take home. If you're considering a small patterned wallcovering, it is worth the expense to buy a whole roll to get an accurate idea of how it will look.

Overall Patterns

*P*erhaps the most engaging pattern of all, overall patterns seem to form a single, tight design. The colors appear to blend together, minimizing the pattern and emphasizing the color. Overall prints are extremely versatile and can be used in any room, either as a dominant element or as a subtle accent. Because overall patterns play tricks on the eye, it is wise to study the pattern—both up close and from a distance—before deciding whether it will work with your decorating scheme.

If your decorating tastes are conservative or you're hesitant about working with patterns, an overall pattern is often a safe option for your decorating scheme. Using more than one overall pattern in a room adds texture and interest and quietly introduces accent colors that tie the scheme together. Overall patterns are also compatible with geometric, large, and small patterns in coordinating hues. They can be featured in the same room with one or more of these other types of patterns, provided the room is balanced with solid- and neutral-toned elements.

Creating a Mood

*I*f you are having trouble deciding on a decorating scheme for a
room, it may help to think about how
you want to feel when you use the room.
For instance, you may want a kitchen that
makes you feel cheerful or a bedroom that
puts you into a relaxed frame of mind.

Each color or combination of colors inspires a
different feeling or mood. Once you have identified
the tone for a room, all you need to do is select the
corresponding hues. Patterns also have a strong effect on the mood of a room.

The following pages feature some popular themes for
rooms and describe the types of colors used to invoke
the mood. There are also suggestions on which types of
rooms are suited for specific moods. The photographs
illustrate these possibilities, giving you ideas for ways
to create mood-inspired decorating schemes.

Bold Schemes

*B*old color schemes are created with high-contrast tones, such as whites and blacks, and complementary hues. Hard-edged geometric patterns and dark walls also contribute to these striking designs. Bold schemes work especially well in entryways and foyers and can also be appropriate in living rooms.

Subtle Schemes

Comfortable, subtle decorating schemes use subdued complementary colors. They often include a careful balance of warm- and cool-toned elements. Subtle schemes are always a safe choice—they are appropriate for any room in your home.

Cheerful Schemes

An airy, cheerful room is created by using light, saturated colors that make the room seem larger. To maintain an open feeling, use low-contrast pastel furnishings and minimal window treatments for maximum sunlight. A cheerful scheme works well in any frequently used room and in children's rooms.

Tranquil Schemes

Using cool related colors that have low contrast is the key to creating a tranquil scheme. To unify the room, use coordinating patterns that repeat the color scheme in draperies, artwork, rugs, and other accents. Use a tranquil scheme in rooms that serve as relaxing retreats.

Formal Schemes

Formal decorating schemes use dark accent colors, rich fabrics, and classically detailed patterns that draw attention. To create a more intimate atmosphere, choose a rich, dark color for the walls. Guest bedrooms, dining rooms, powder rooms, and parlors are all well suited for a formal decorating scheme.

Natural Schemes

Warm earth tones with simple patterns and textures are the basis of natural schemes. Often, the warmth of brown tones is balanced with light cool colors, such as blue and gray. Libraries and family rooms often feature a natural scheme.

Finalizing a Room Design

*A*fter you have chosen a color scheme and a mood for a room, you are ready to select the paint, wallcovering, and fabrics to complete your decorating scheme. The information in this section will help you sort through and organize samples and show you how to make the best selections.

In this section, you will learn how to save time and simplify decisions by working with coordinated collections of fabrics, wallcoverings, and borders. Although they can cost more than other materials, coordinates are an easy way to create a professional-looking room.

This section also shows you how to work with existing elements, such as countertops, floor coverings, and plumbing fixtures, and how to incorporate them into the new decorating plan. You will also learn how to collect samples of your existing elements to take along when selecting paint, wallcovering, and other treatments.

Narrowing your selections down to a few samples at the decorating center can be a difficult task. On the following pages, you'll learn methods used by professional decorating consultants to narrow their choices, and how to select a handful of samples to take home for closer consideration.

You will also find some tried-and-true methods for testing samples in the rooms you plan to redecorate. These will help you get a realistic idea of how specific shades of paint, wallcoverings, and fabric will look when the decorating process is completed.

Coordinated Collections

Coordinated collections of fabrics, wallcoverings, and borders give you great flexibility in designing a room. By using the same fabric in draperies, pillows, and furniture slipcovers, you can unify a room.

These collections offer more flexibility than you might imagine. Working with coordinates, you can create a low-contrast, high-contrast, or multipattern scheme in a room. Each of these schemes will have a different effect on the look and feel of a room.

Low-contrast Scheme

A single pattern in the fabric unifies the draperies and furniture. Here, the wall color was chosen to match the light background color in the fabric. This makes the room seem larger by helping the furniture blend into the walls. Repeating the same pattern will help unify adjoining rooms.

High-contrast Scheme

The dark green in the fabric is used as the background wall color to form a strong contrast with the light carpeting and upholstery fabrics. The detailed pattern in the wallcovering border contrasts with the solid colors surrounding it.

Multipattern Scheme

Several different patterns can be combined successfully in the same room. The different patterns in this room are unified by related floral designs and repeated colors. The wallcovering border helps blend the room elements together.

Working with Existing Colors

You may find it necessary to base the color scheme of a room on existing surfaces or fixtures that you are not replacing, such as tiles or carpet, or a colored tub, sink, or toilet. Countertops are other elements that are often retained because they are expensive to replace.

An easy way to blend these permanent fixtures into the new look of a room is by choosing paint colors and wallcovering that carry more visual weight than the old fixture.

If the existing surfaces are pastel or neutral, you can draw attention away from them by introducing stronger or brighter colors in the room. For example, if porcelain fixtures in a bathroom are mint green, you might select a patterned wallcovering that is predominately forest green. If the existing colors are bright, you can soften their impact with the addition of calm colors.

You can also mimic the existing colors in subtle features of a wallcovering or in small accessories, such as a soap dish or a telephone. This can make the old fixture or surface appear as a legitimate element of the decorating plan.

Tips for Working with Existing Colors

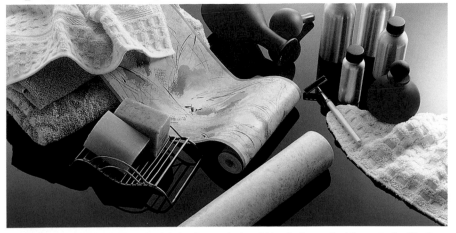

Bright fixtures (cobalt blue, in this bathroom) should be balanced with neutrals. To tie in the bold fixtures, add small accessories in the bright hue.

This color sample represents the existing bright blue porcelain fixtures.

Pastel fixtures, such as a light green tub, sink, and toilet, draw less attention when they are surrounded by brighter or darker shades of the same color. Shown here, darker greens have been used with light green fixtures. Yellow accessories are used as accents.

This color sample represents the existing green porcelain fixtures.

Gray floor tiles can be balanced by adding accessories in striking colors. Shown here, black, white, and red are used to accessorize a room, with touches of gray in the wallcovering.

This color sample represents the existing gray tiles.

Paint & Wallcovering Selection

When you begin shopping for a new paint color or wallcovering, bring fabric swatches and other samples of your home furnishings to the decorating center. Photographs of a room can give you and others a helpful perspective of the room's layout and architectural features.

Many decorating centers have professional design consultants who help customers at no charge. The paint selection display in a home decorating center can hold more than a thousand different colors, and wallcovering departments may have several hundred sample books. By comparing the samples from your home with the store's paint swatches and wallcovering samples, you can narrow your selections quickly.

Always bring several paint or wallcovering samples back to your home for a day or two before making a final selection. Look at the samples in the room you are decorating to see how the colors and patterns interact with the existing furnishings. Remember that colors change under different lighting conditions, so follow the 24-hour test on page 57.

Tips for Selecting Paint & Wallcovering

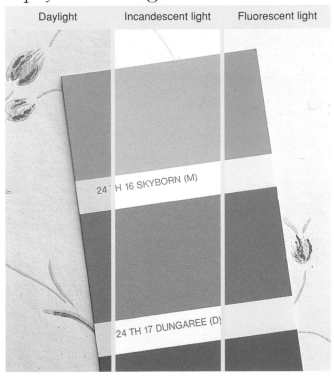

Daylight   Incandescent light   Fluorescent light

24 TH 16 SKYBORN (M)

24 TH 17 DUNGAREE (D)

In the store, check paint chips and wallcovering samples in daylight, as well as under artificial lighting. And remember that store lighting can differ from home lighting.

Take home no more than three different color and wallcovering samples. Fewer alternatives make the final decision easier.

Look at the dark end of a paint chip card to determine the tint base of an off-white paint. Almost all off-white hues contain a hint of another color.

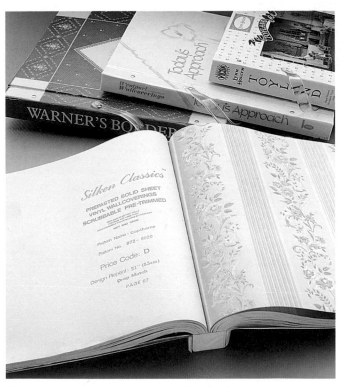

Choose wallcovering books by quickly flipping through them. A quick glance saves time and can tell you which books you will want to study more carefully.

(continued next page)

Tips for Selecting Paint & Wallcovering (continued)

Tape four paint chips together. Larger color samples are easier to judge. Cut off the white borders, which can be distracting.

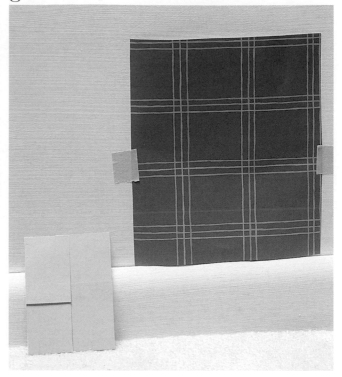

Judge samples of paint and wallcovering in the room where they will be used. Stand color samples upright to duplicate the way light strikes a wall surface. Tape wallcovering samples against the walls where they will be hung.

Before making a final decision, cut a large sample of wallcovering to use in the 24-hour test (opposite page). Decorating centers will usually provide large samples or let you borrow sample books.

Buy a quart of your chosen paint color. Paint a large sample card to hang on the wall. Follow the 24-hour test (opposite page) before buying the full amounts of paint and wallcovering needed.

The 24-Hour Test

Lighting affects color. To judge how paint or wall-covering will look in a specific area, hang a large sample on the wall and check it from time to time over the course of a full day. Notice how the color changes under varying lighting situations. If a room is most often used at a particular time of day, look at the color carefully at this time. Paint and wallcovering colors will look different in your home than they do in the decorating center. Furniture, woodwork, and floors reflect their own colors onto the walls, changing their appearance.

Incandescent indoor lighting generally has a yellow cast, although the choice of lightbulb and shade can change its tint.

Natural daylight has a blue cast at midday but has a warm orange tint at sunrise and sunset.

Basic Painting
& Wallcovering

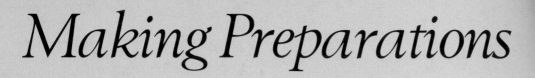

Making Preparations

*P*reparation is the key to ensuring the success of a painting or wallcovering project. The preparation process includes selecting the proper tools, removing or covering items that need protection, repairing walls and ceilings, repairing woodwork, masking and draping, and applying primers.

In this section, you will learn how to choose the tools and materials you'll need for preparation—the items favored by professional painters. You will also learn many time-saving "tricks of the trade" that will help you work more efficiently.

The guidelines outlined for preparing a room provide an easy-to-follow plan for protecting furniture, hardware, and fixtures from unwanted paint splatters.

Blemished walls must be given a new, smooth surface before they can accept paint or wallcovering.

Ladders & Scaffolds

Two quality stepladders and an extension plank are all you need to paint most interior surfaces. For painting high areas, build a simple scaffold by running the plank through the steps of two stepladders. It can be easy to lose your balance or step off the plank, so choose tall ladders for safety; the upper part of the ladders can help you balance and will keep you from stepping off the ends of the plank. Buy a strong, straight 2" × 10" board no more than 12 feet long, or rent a plank from a material dealer or rental outlet.

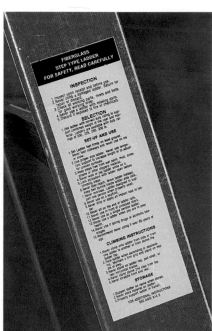

A manufacturer's sticker provides weight ratings and instructions for the correct use of the ladder. Read it carefully when shopping for a ladder. Choose a ladder that will easily accommodate your weight plus the additional weight of any tools or materials you plan to carry up the ladder.

How to Make a Scaffold

For ceilings and high spots on walls, make a simple scaffold by running an extension plank through the steps of two stepladders. The plank should be no more than 12 feet long. The ladders should face away from each other, so that the steps are on the inside of the scaffold. Make sure the ladder braces are down and locked, and watch your footing.

How to Use a Scaffold in Stairways

For stairs, run an extension plank through the step of a ladder, and place the other end on a stairway step. Make sure the ladder is steady, and check to see that the plank is level. Keep the plank close to the wall, if possible, and never overreach.

Tips for Using Ladders & Scaffolds

Rent extension planks from a paint dealer or from a rental center.

Choose straight planks without large knots or cracks. Choose 2" × 10" boards that have some spring in them: old, brittle wooden planks can break unexpectedly.

Push braces completely down and make certain they are locked. Legs of the ladder should be level and steady against the ground.

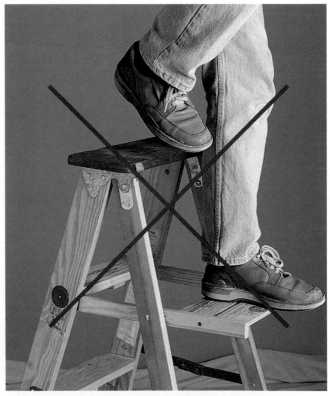

Do not stand on the top step, top brace, or utility shelf of a stepladder.

Center your weight on the ladder. Move the ladder often: do not overreach.

Keep steps tight by periodically checking them and tightening the braces when they need it.

Keep the ladder in front of you when working. Lean your body against the ladder for balance.

An adjustable ladder adapts to many different work needs. It can be used as a straight ladder, a stepladder, or a base for scaffold planks.

Preparation Tools & Materials

*I*t's as simple as it is unavoidable: Good preparation produces a professional-looking job. In the old days, preparation could be difficult and time consuming, but with the help of the new tools and materials on the market today, it's easier than ever.

New cleaners and removal agents help prepare surfaces for paint and wallcovering; new patching products help you create virtually invisible wall repairs; ingenious new masking and draping materials take the tedium out of keeping the paint where it belongs; primers and sealers provide good coverage and help paint bond properly. While you're in the planning stages of a painting or decorating project, take a stroll down the aisles at a local home center or hardware store. Consider the project ahead of you and evaluate which products will make the job simpler and more enjoyable.

Tools for preparation include some ordinary home workshop tools and some specialty items. All are available at home improvement centers, as well as at better decorating supply stores.

Smooth, even surfaces are easy to achieve with tools such as these: sanding sponges (A), sandpaper (B), sanding block (C), a drywall-corner sanding sponge (D), microfiber tack cloth (E), and synthetic steel wool (F).

Wall repair materials include: self-adhesive seam tape (A), hole-patching kits (B), crack-repair compound (C), joint compound (D), stainblocking primer/sealer (E), and sink and tub caulk (F). Some new spackling compounds (G) start out pink and dry white so you can see when they're ready to be sanded and painted. Sponges (H) are useful for smoothing damp joint compound to reduce the amount of sanding that's necessary later.

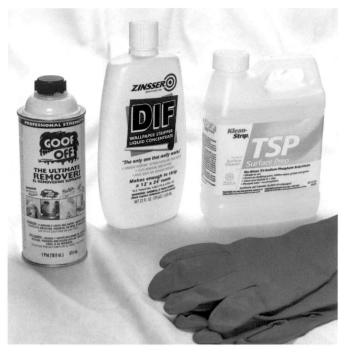

Walls must be clean, smooth, and free of grease before a painting project. If wallpaper is to be removed, a wallpaper removal agent is extremely helpful. Clockwise from top left are: cleanup solution to remove old drips and splatters, wallcovering remover to strip old wallcoverings, Trisodium Phosphate (TSP) for washing the walls, and rubber gloves, which should be worn when using chemicals such as these.

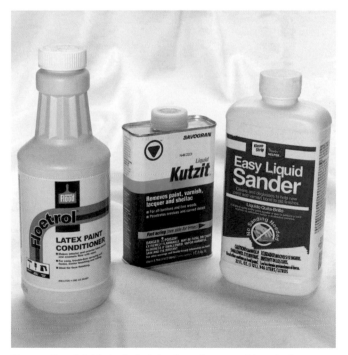

Preparation liquids include latex bonding agent for plaster repairs; paint remover; and liquid deglosser, for dulling glossy surfaces prior to painting.

Primers provide maximum adhesion for paint on any surface. There are many specialty primers available, including mold-resistant primers that are especially useful in areas that tend to be damp, such as bathrooms (A), primers made for plaster and new drywall (B), stainblocking primers (C), and tinted primers that reduce the need for multiple coats of paint (particularly for deep colors) (D).

Making Preparations 67

Room Preparation

How to Prepare a Room

*B*efore painting, your first step is to protect everything that could be covered by dust or splattered by paint.Remove all window and door hardware, light fixtures, and coverplates on outlets and wall switches. Drape furniture and cover the floors. Remove heating and air conditioning duct covers. Mask off wood moldings with self-adhesive paper or masking tape.

Tip:

When removing hardware, mark the pieces with masking tape for identification so that they can easily be replaced.

1 Remove all hardware, such as window handles and cabinet catches, from surfaces to be painted. If you will be installing new hardware, buy it now and drill new screw holes if needed.

2 Remove all nails, screws, and picture hangers from surfaces to be painted. To prevent damage to the plaster or wallboard, use a block of wood under the head of the hammer.

3 Remove covers from heating and air-conditioning ducts to protect them from splatters. Remove thermostats, or use masking tape to protect them against paint drips.

4 Move furniture to the center of the room and cover it with plastic sheets. In large rooms, leave an alley through the center for access if you are painting the ceiling. Cover floors with 9-ounce canvas drop cloths. Canvas absorbs paint spills.

5 Turn off the electricity. Remove the coverplates from outlets and switches, then replace the cover screws. Lower light fixtures away from electrical boxes, or remove the fixtures. Cover hanging fixtures with plastic bags.

Wallcovering Removal

Newer vinyl wallcoverings often can be peeled off by hand. Some will leave a paper and adhesive residue that is easily removed with water. With nonpeelable wallcoverings, pierce the surface with a perforation tool, then apply a remover solution to dissolve the adhesive.

Wallcovering remover fluids contain wetting agents that penetrate the paper and help soften the adhesive. Use a remover solution to wash away old adhesive after wallcovering is removed.

If the old wallcovering was hung over unsealed wallboard, it may be impossible to remove it without destroying the wallboard. You may be able to paint or hang new wallcovering directly over the old wallcovering, but the surface should be smooth and primed. Before painting over wallcovering, prime with alkyd wallboard primer.

How to Remove Wallcovering

Find a loose edge and try to strip off the wallcovering. Vinyls often peel away easily.

1 If the wallcovering does not strip by hand, cover the floor with layers of newspaper. Add wallcovering remover fluid to a bucket of water, as directed by the manufacturer.

2 Pierce the wallcovering surface with a perforation tool. This allows the remover solution to enter and soften the adhesive.

3 Use a pressure sprayer, paint roller, or sponge to apply the remover solution. Let it soak into the covering, according to the manufacturer's directions.

4 Peel away loosened wallcovering with a 6" wallboard knife. Be careful not to damage the plaster or wallboard. Remove all backing paper.

5 Rinse adhesive residue from the wall with remover solution. Rinse with clear water and let the walls dry completely.

Ceiling & Wall Repairs

*T*horoughly washing, rinsing, and sanding your walls before priming them will guarantee a long-lasting finish. For a professional appearance, carefully check your walls for damage and repair the wallboard or plaster as needed. Pregummed fiberglass wallboard tapes and premixed patching compounds reduce drying time and let you patch and paint a wall the same day.

Wash and sand before repainting. Use a TSP (trisodium phosphate) solution and a sponge to cut grease and to remove dirt. Wear rubber gloves and wash walls from the bottom up, using a damp sponge, to avoid streaks. Rinse thoroughly with clean water. After drying, lightly sand surfaces.

How to Remove Stains

1 Apply stain remover to a clean, dry cloth and rub lightly to remove the stain.

2 Seal all stain areas with white pigmented shellac. Pigmented shellac prevents stains from bleeding through the new paint.

3 Water or rust stains may indicate water damage. Check for leaking pipes and soft plaster, make needed repairs, then seal the area with stain-killing sealer.

How to Remove Mildew

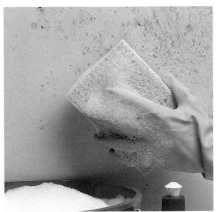

1 Test stains by washing with water and detergent. Mildew stains will not wash out.

2 Wearing rubber gloves and eye protection, wash the walls with bleach, which kills mildew spores.

3 After the bleach treatment, wash away mildew with a TSP solution, and rinse with clear water.

How to Patch Peeling Paint

1 Scrape away loose paint with a putty knife or paint scraper.

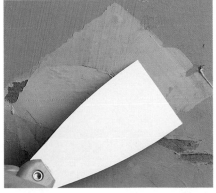

2 Apply spackle to the edges of chipped paint with a putty knife or flexible wallboard knife.

3 Sand the patch area with 150-grit production sandpaper. The patch area should feel smooth to the touch.

How to Fill Nail Holes

1 Apply lightweight spackle to holes with a putty knife or your fingertip. This keeps repair areas small, so they are easy to hide with paint. Let the spackle dry.

2 Lightly sand the repair area with 150-grit production sandpaper. Production paper has an open surface that does not clog easily. Wipe away dust with a damp sponge, then prime the spot with PVA primer.

How to Fill Shallow Dents & Holes

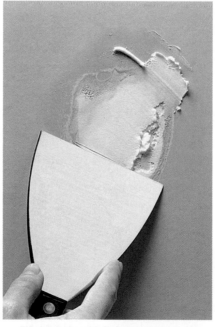

1 Scrape or sand away any loose plaster, peeled paint, or wallboard face paper to ensure a solid base for patching.

2 Fill the hole with lightweight spackle. Apply the spackle with the smallest wallboard knife that will span the entire hole. Let the spackle dry.

3 Lightly sand the area with 150-grit production sandpaper.

How to Fix Popped Wallboard Nails

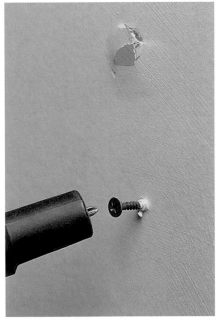

1 Drive a wallboard screw 2" away from popped nail. Be sure the screw hits a stud or joist and pulls the wallboard tight against the framing.

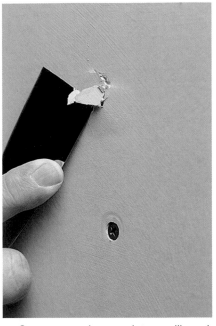

2 Scrape away loose paint or wallboard compound. Drive the popped nail back into the framing so the head is sunk ¹⁄₁₆" below the surface of the wallboard. Do not set the nail with a punch.

3 Use a wallboard knife to apply 3 coats of premixed wallboard compound to the nail and screw holes, letting it dry between coats. Sand and prime the patched area.

How to Repair Cracks in Plaster

1 Scrape away any texture or loose plaster around the crack. Reinforce the crack with pregummed fiberglass wallboard tape.

2 Use a taping knife or trowel to apply spackle or wallboard compound to cover over the tape so the tape is just concealed: if compound is too thick, it will recrack.

3 Apply a second thin coat if necessary to conceal the tape edges. Sand lightly and prime the repair area. Retexture the surface (pages 112–113).

How to Patch Small Holes in Wallboard

1 Inspect the damaged area. If there are no cracks around the edge of the hole, just fill the hole with spackle, let it dry, and sand the area smooth.

2 If the edges are cracked, cover the hole with a peel-and-stick repair patch. The patch has a metal mesh center for strength, and can be cut or shaped as needed. Patches are available in several sizes.

3 Use a wallboard knife to cover the patch with spackle or wallboard compound. Two coats may be needed. Let the patch set until it is nearly dry.

4 Use a damp sponge or wallboard wet sander to smooth the repair area. This eliminates dust caused by dry sanding.

How to Patch Larger Holes in Wallboard

1 Outline the damaged area with a framing square. Use a wallboard saw or jig saw to cut away the damaged section.

2 Install wood or wallboard backer strips. For wood, use a wallboard screw gun and 1¼" wallboard screws to secure the strip in place.

Or, use wallboard backers secured by hot glue as an alternative to wood backer strips. Cut a wallboard patch to size, then screw or glue the wallboard patch in place over the backer strips.

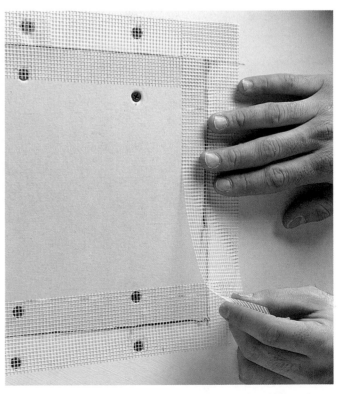

3 Apply wallboard tape to the cracks, then apply wallboard compound and wet-sand the area (opposite page).

Repairing Holes in Plaster

Modern repair methods and materials have simplified the job of repairing holes in plaster. Coating the patch area with latex bonding liquid ensures a good bond and a tight, crack-free patch. Bonding liquid also eliminates the need to wet the plaster and lath to prevent premature drying and shrinkage. Ask your hardware dealer for a good concrete/plaster latex bonding liquid.

How to Repair Holes in Plaster

1 Sand or scrape any textured paint from the area around the hole.

2 Test with a scraper to be sure the plaster is solid and tight around the damaged area. Scrape away any loose or soft plaster.

3 Apply latex bonding liquid liberally around the edges of the hole and over the base lath to ensure a crack-free bond between the old and new plaster.

4 Mix patching plaster as directed by the manufacturer, and use a wallboard knife or trowel to apply it to the hole. Fill shallow holes with a single coat of plaster.

5 For deeper holes, apply a shallow first coat, then scratch a crosshatch pattern in the wet plaster. Let it dry, then apply second coat of plaster. Let the plaster dry, and sand it lightly.

6 Use texture paint or wallboard compound to recreate any surface texture, as directed on pages 112–113.

Paint Removal for Wood

B efore painting or refinishing, wood should be cleaned, repaired, and sanded. If the old paint is heavily layered or badly chipped, it should be stripped before the wood is repainted.

If you are using a heat gun to strip wood, take care not to scorch the wood. Never use a heat gun after using chemical strippers: the chemical residue may be vaporized or ignited by the heat.

When using a chemical paint stripper, always wear protective clothing and safety gear, including eye protection and a respirator. Follow the label directions for safe use, and always work in a well-ventilated area.

How to Use Chemical Stripper

1 Follow label directions for the safe use of chemicals. Wear heavy rubber gloves and eye protection, use drop cloths, and open windows and doors for ventilation when working with chemical strippers.

2 Apply a liberal coat of stripper to painted wood with a paint brush or steel wool. Let it stand until the paint begins to blister. Do not let the stripper dry out on wood surfaces.

3 Scrape away the paint with a putty knife or scraper and steel wool as soon as it softens. Rub the stripped wood with denatured alcohol and new steel wool to help clean the grain. Wipe the wood with a wet sponge or solvent, as directed on the stripper label.

How to Use a Heat Gun

1 Hold the heat gun near the wood until the paint softens and just begins to blister. Overheating can make the paint gummy and may scorch the wood. Always be careful when using a heat gun around flammable materials.

2 Remove softened paint with a scraper or putty knife. Scrapers are available in many shapes for removing paint from shaped moldings. Sand away any paint residue remaining after heat stripping.

Woodwork Patching

For the best results, woodwork should be cleaned, patched and sanded before it is re-painted. A liquid deglosser helps to dull shiny sur-faces so they will bond with new paint. If new hardware is to be installed, check to see if new pieces will fit old screw holes. If new screw holes must be drilled, fill the old holes with wood patcher.

To renew varnished wood, clean the surfaces with mineral spirits or furniture refinisher, then patch any holes with a wood patcher that is tinted to match the existing finish. Sand the wood smooth, and apply one or two coats of varnish.

How to Prepare for Painting

1 Wash woodwork with TSP solution, and rinse. Scrape away any peeling or loose paint. Badly chipped woodwork should be stripped (pages 80–81).

How to Prepare for Refinishing

1 Clean woodwork with a soft cloth and odorless mineral spirits or liquid furniture refinisher.

2 Use a putty knife to apply latex wood patch or spackle to any nail holes, dents, and any other damaged areas.

3 Sand the surfaces with 150-grit production paper until they are smooth to the touch. Wipe woodwork with a tack cloth before priming and painting.

2 Apply wood patch to holes and dents with a putty knife. Sand patch areas lightly with 150-grit production sandpaper.

3 Apply a clear wood sealer to the patch area (page 89). Restain the area to match the surrounding wood. Apply one or two coats of varnish.

Masking & Draping

*F*or fast, mess-free painting, shield any surfaces that could get splattered. If you are painting only the ceiling, drape the walls and woodwork to prevent splatters. When painting walls, mask the baseboards and the window and door casings.

While the tried-and-true method of aligning painter's tape with the edge of moldings and casings is perfectly adequate, the job goes much faster and smoother with a tape applicator. Similarly, painter's tape can be used to cover door hinges and window glass, but hinge masks and corner masks simplify the job enormously. Evaluate the available choices and the project at hand: There are many new, easy-to-use options available.

Before beginning to mask and drape the room, remove lightweight furniture and move heavier pieces to the center of the room. Cover the furniture and then the floor with heavy canvas or plastic drop cloths.

Masking and draping materials simplify the process of protecting surrounding surfaces: plastic and canvas drop cloths (A), adhesive corner masks (B), masking and painting tape applicator (C), and painter's tape (D).

How to Drape Walls

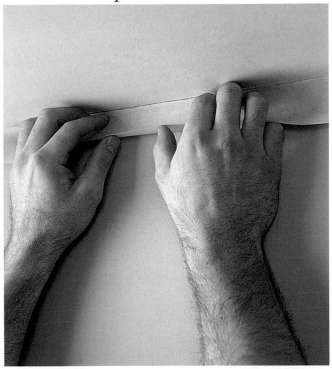

1 Press the top half of 2" masking tape along the joint between the ceiling and the wall. Leave the bottom half of the masking tape loose.

2 Hang sheet plastic under masking tape, draping the walls and baseboards. After painting, remove the loose edge as soon as the paint is too dry to run.

How to Mask Wood Trim

1 Align wide masking tape with the inside edge of the molding; press in place. Run the tip of a putty knife along the inside edge of the tape to seal it against seeping paint. After painting, remove the tape as soon as the paint is too dry to run.

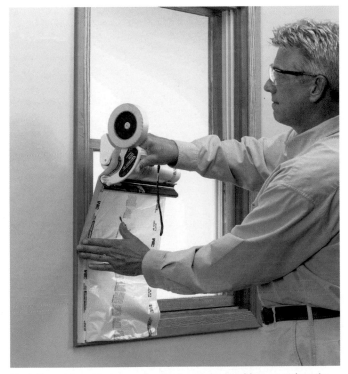

Variation: Use a tape applicator to apply masking or painter's tape. Hold the applicator against the wood, hold the edge of the tape, and move the applicator along the surface of the trim. The applicator presses the tape in place.

Final Check & Cleanup

Before painting, make a final check of the work area. Clean the room thoroughly to eliminate dust that might collect on tools and settle on wet paint. Maintain the temperature and humidity levels recommended by product labels. This will help keep paint edges wet while painting, minimizing lap marks in the finished job.

It is also important for the paint to dry within normal time limits so dirt can't settle on the finish while it is wet. When applying wallcovering, a proper work climate prevents the adhesive from drying prematurely, which can cause blisters or loose edges on the wallcovering.

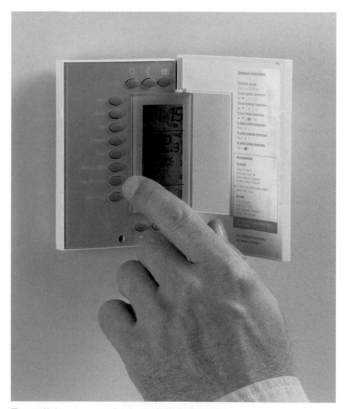

Check all surfaces to be painted with a strong sidelight. Sand, or spackle and sand, any rough spots that were missed in preparation.

Turn off thermostats for forced-air furnaces and air conditioners so that the fan will not circulate dust through the area being painted.

Sand all surfaces that will be painted with 150-grit production sandpaper. Sanding dulls the surface so it will accept new paint. Wipe walls with a tack rag.

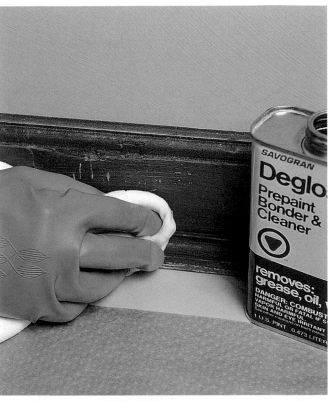

Wipe dust from woodwork with a tack rag, or with a clean cloth moistened with liquid deglosser.

Use a vacuum cleaner to pick up the dust from windowsills and window tracks, and from baseboards and casements.

If humidity levels are low, place a humidifier in the room before painting or wallcovering. This keeps paint or adhesive from drying too fast.

Primers & Sealers

A sealer should be applied to wood surfaces before they are varnished. Wood often has both hard and soft grains, as well as a highly absorbent end grain. Applying a sealer helps close the surface of the wood so the varnish is absorbed evenly in different types of wood grain. If the wood is not sealed, the varnish may dry to a mottled finish.

Primers are used to seal surfaces that will be painted. Wallboard seams and patched areas absorb paint at a different rate than surrounding areas. Joints and patch areas often show or "shadow" through the finished paint if the walls are not adequately primed.

Choose a primer designed for the project: mildew-resistant primers are excellent for bathrooms and laundry rooms, stain-blocking primers cover smoke and other hard-to-cover stains, and tinted primers provide good bases for deep colors, such as red or purple.

Tinted primers provide an excellent base for finish coats, especially for deep colors that might otherwise require several coats to cover adequately. Color base is available to tint white primers if necessary.

Paint Safety

*A*lways read and follow the label information on paint and solvent containers. Chemicals that pose a fire hazard are listed (in order of flammability) as: combustible, flammable, or extremely flammable. Use caution when using these products and remember that the fumes are also flammable.

The warning "use with adequate ventilation" means that there should be no more vapor buildup than there would be if you were using the material outside. Open doors and windows, use exhaust fans, and wear an approved respirator if you can't provide adequate ventilation.

Save a small amount of paint for touchups and repairs, and then safely dispose of the remainder. Dispose of alkyd (oil-based) paint according to local regulations regarding hazardous materials; if possible, recycle latex paint at your local hazardous waste disposal facility or allow it to dry out completely and set it out with your regular trash.

Paint chemicals do not store well. Buy only as much as is needed for the project and keep them away from children and pets.

Read label information. Chemicals that are poisonous or flammable are labeled with warnings and instructions for safe handling.

Wear safety goggles when using chemical stripper or cleaning products. Use goggles when painting overhead.

Do not use chemicals that are listed as combustible or flammable, such as paint strippers, near an open flame. Store paint chemicals out of the reach of children and away from appliances with pilot lights, such as a furnace or gas oven.

Open windows and doors and use a fan for ventilation when painting indoors. If a product label has the warning "harmful or fatal if swallowed," assume that the vapors are dangerous to breathe.

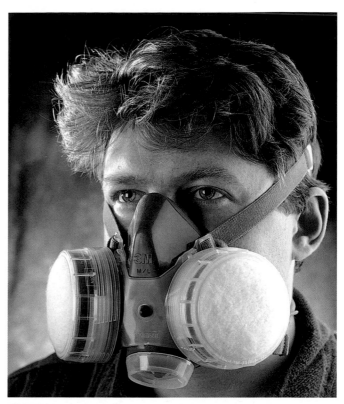

Wear a respirator to filter vapors if you cannot ventilate a work area adequately. If you can smell vapors, the ventilation is not adequate.

Pour paint thinner into a clear jar after use. When the solid material settles out, pour off the clear thinner and save it to reuse later. Dispose of the sediment as hazardous waste.

Dispose of leftover latex primers and paint safely. Let the container stand uncovered until the paint dries completely. In most communities, dried latex paint can be put into the regular trash. (Alkyd primers and paint must be disposed of as hazardous waste.)

Paint Selection

*P*aints are either water-base (latex) or alkyd-base. Latex paint is easy to apply and clean up, and the improved chemistry of today's latexes makes them suitable for nearly everyapplication. Some painters feel that alkyd paint allows for a smoother finished surface, but local regulations may restrict the use of alkyd-base products.

Paints come in various sheens. Paint finishes range from flat to high-gloss enamels. Gloss enamels dry to a shiny finish, and are used for surfaces that need to be washed often, like walls in bathrooms and kitchens, and for woodwork. Flat paints are used for most wall and ceiling applications.

Paint prices typically are an accurate reflection of quality. As a general rule, buy the best paint your budget can afford. High-quality paints are easier to use and they look better than cheaper paints. And because quality paints last longer and cover better than budget paints, often requiring fewer coats, they are usually less expensive in the long run.

Always use a good primer to coat surfaces before painting. The primer bonds well to all surfaces and provides a durable base that helps keep the finish coat from cracking or peeling. When using deep colors, choose a tinted primer to reduce the number of coats of paint necessary to achieve good coverage.

How to Estimate Paint

1) Length of wall or ceiling (feet)	
2) Height of wall, or width of ceiling	×
3) Surface area	=
4) Coverage per gallon of chosen paint	÷
5) Gallons of paint needed	=

How to Select a Quality Paint

Paint coverage (listed on can labels) of quality paint should be about 400 square feet per gallon. Bargain paints (left) may require two or even three coats to cover the same area as quality paints.

High washability is a feature of quality paint. The pigments in bargain paints (right) may "chalk" and wash away with mild scrubbing.

Paint Sheens

Paint comes in a variety of surface finishes, or sheens. Gloss enamel (A) provides a highly reflective finish for areas where high washability is important. All gloss paints tend to show surface flaws. Alkyd-base enamels have the highest gloss. Medium-gloss latex enamel creates a highly washable surface with a slightly less reflective finish. Like gloss enamels, medium-gloss paints (B) tend to show surface flaws. Eggshell enamel (C) combines the soft finish with the washability of enamel. Flat latex (D) is an all-purpose paint with a soft finish that hides surface irregularities.

Tools & Equipment

Most painting jobs can be done with a few quality tools. Purchase two or three premium brushes, a sturdy paint pan that can be attached to a stepladder, a supply of disposable pan liners, and a variety of roller covers. With proper care, high-quality brushes will last for years.

Brushes made of hog or ox bristles should be used only with alkyd-base paints. All-purpose brushes blend polyester, nylon, and sometimes animal bristles. Choose a straight-edged 3" wall brush, a 2" straight-edged trim brush, and a tapered sash brush.

How to Choose a Paintbrush

Chiseled end

Flagged bristles

Spacer plugs

Reinforced ferrule

Hardwood handle

A quality brush (left), has a shaped hardwood handle and a sturdy reinforced ferrule made of noncorrosive metal. Multiple spacer plugs separate the bristles. A quality brush has flagged (split) bristles and a chiseled end for precise edging. A cheaper brush (right) will have a blunt end, unflagged bristles, and a cardboard spacer plug that may soften when wet.

A 3" straight-edged brush (top) is a good choice for cutting paint lines at ceilings and in corners. For painting woodwork, a 2" trim brush (middle) works well. Choose brushes with chiseled tips for painting in corners. A tapered sash brush (bottom) can help when painting corners on window sashes.

Paint Rollers & Roller Accessories

A good roller frame is an inexpensive, time-saving tool that can last for years. Choose a well-balanced frame with nylon bearings and a comfortable handle with a threaded end that accepts an extension handle.

Roller covers are available in a wide variety of materials and nap lengths. Most jobs can be done with ⅜" nap. Select medium-priced synthetic roller covers that can be reused a few times before being discarded. Bargain roller covers might shed fibers onto the painted surface, and cannot be cleaned or reused. Rinse all roller covers before use to remove lint.

Use more expensive lamb's wool roller covers when using most alkyd-based paints. Mohair covers work well with gloss alkyd paints, where complete smoothness is important.

Synthetic covers (left) are good with most paints, especially latexes. Wool or mohair roller covers (right) give an even finish with alkyd products. Choose good-quality roller covers, which will be less likely to shed lint.

Select the proper roller cover for the surface you intend to paint. A ¼"-nap cover is used for very flat surfaces. A ⅜"-nap cover will cover the small flaws found in most flat walls and ceilings. A 1"-nap cover fills spaces in rough surfaces, such as concrete blocks or stucco walls. Foam rollers fit into small spaces and work well when painting furniture or doing touch-ups. Corner rollers have nap on the ends and make it easy to paint corners without cutting in the edges.

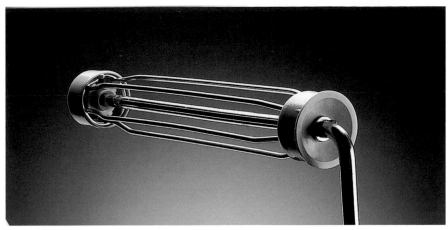

Choose a sturdy roller with a wire cage construction. Nylon bearings should roll smoothly and easily when you spin the cage. The handle end should be threaded for attaching an extension handle.

Buy a paint tray with legs that allow the tray to sit steadily on the shelf of a ladder. Disposable tray liners simplify clean up: simply allow the paint to dry completely and throw the liner away in the regular trash. Look for a textured ramp that keeps the roller turning easily.

A five-gallon paint container and paint screen speed up the process of painting large areas. Some manufacturers offer containers with built-in roller trays that let you paint straight from the container. Do not try to balance a five-gallon container on the shelf of a ladder—it's too heavy.

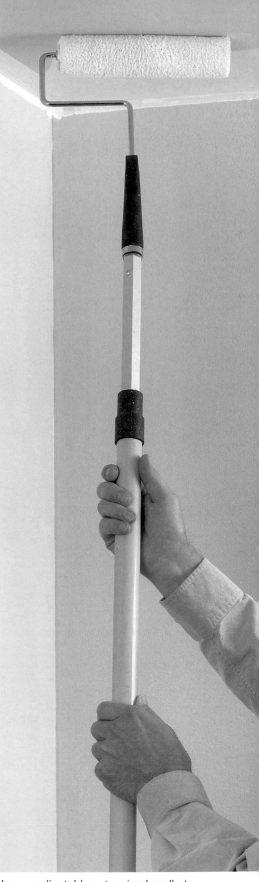

Use an adjustable extension handle to paint ceilings and tall walls easily without a ladder.

Specialty Painting Tools

*S*urfaces with unusual angles and contours are sometimes difficult to paint with standard rollers and brushes. Specialty tools make some painting situations easier. Disposable foam brushes, for instance, are excellent for applying an even coat of clear varnish to smooth woodwork, and paint gloves make painting contoured surfaces a much simpler task.

An airless paint sprayer is useful for painting large areas or for irregular surfaces, like louvered closet doors. All sprayers produce some overspray, so wear protective gear and mask off all areas likely to be splattered. Movable workpieces should be painted outside or in your basement or garage. Thinning the paint before spraying will result in easier use of the tool and more even coverage.

Specialty roller covers, available in a variety of light and heavy textures, make it easy to achieve a consistent, textured surface.

A bendable tool can be shaped to fit unusual surfaces, such as window shutters or the fins of cast-iron radiators.

A paint glove simplifies painting of pipes and other contoured surfaces, like wrought iron.

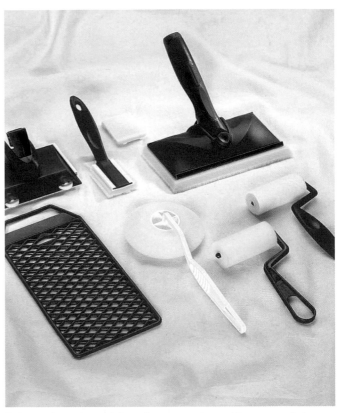

Paint pads and specialty rollers come in a wide range of sizes and shapes to fit different painting needs.

Aerosol spray paint speeds the painting of any small, intricate jobs, like heat registers.

A paint mixer bit attaches to a power drill to stir paints quickly and easily. Use a variable-speed drill at low speed to avoid air bubbles in the paint.

Mix paint together (called "boxing") in a large pail to eliminate slight color variations between cans. Stir the paint thoroughly with a wooden stick or power drill attachment. To keep paint from building up in the groove around the paint can lid, pound several small nail holes into the groove. This allows the paint to drip back into the can.

Basic Painting Methods

For a professional-looking paint job, spread the paint evenly onto the work surface without letting it run, drip, or lap onto other areas. Excess paint will run on the surface and can drip onto woodwork and floors. Stretching paint too far leaves lap marks and results in patchy coverage.

Start each section by "cutting in" with a brush on all edges, corners, and trim. Painting flat surfaces with brushes and rollers is a three-step process. First, apply the paint to the work surface, then distribute it evenly. Finally, smooth it out for a seamless finish.

How to Use a Paint Brush

1 Dip the brush, loading one-third of its bristle length. Tap the bristles against the side of the can. Dipping deeper overloads the brush. Dragging the brush against the lip of the can causes the bristles to wear.

2 Cut in the edges using the narrow edge of the brush, pressing just enough to flex the bristles. Keep an eye on the paint edge, and paint with long, slow strokes. Always paint from a dry area back into wet paint to avoid lap marks.

3 Brush wall corners using the wide edge of the brush. Paint open areas with a brush or roller before the brushed paint dries.

4 To paint large areas with a brush, apply the paint with 2 or 3 diagonal strokes. Hold the brush at a 45° angle to the work surface, pressing just enough to flex the bristles. Distribute the paint evenly with horizontal strokes.

5 Smooth the surface by drawing the brush vertically from the top to the bottom of the painted area. Use light strokes and lift the brush from the surface at the end of each stroke. This method is best for slow-drying alkyd enamels.

Roller Techniques

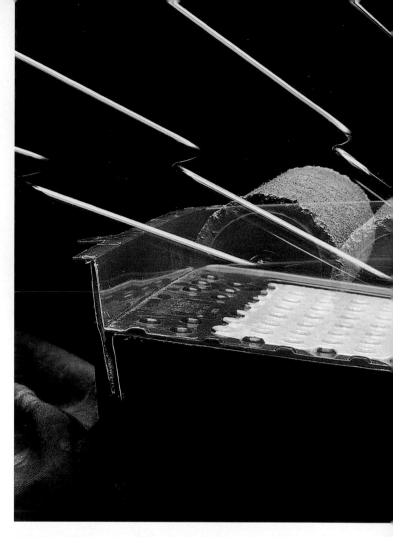

*P*aint surfaces in small sections, working from dry surfaces back into wet paint to avoid roller marks. If a paint job takes more than a day, cover the roller tightly with plastic wrap or store it in a bucket of water overnight to prevent the paint from drying out.

Wet the roller cover with water (when painting with latex paint) or mineral spirits (when painting with alkyd enamel), to remove lint and prime the roller cover.

How to Paint With a Paint Roller

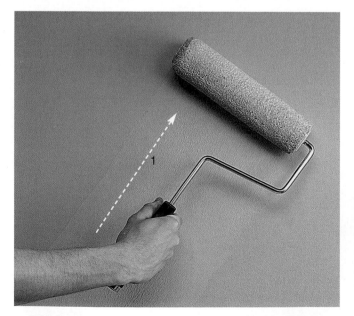

1 With the loaded roller, make a diagonal sweep (1) about 4' long on the surface. On walls, roll upward on the first stroke to avoid spilling paint. Use slow roller strokes to avoid splattering.

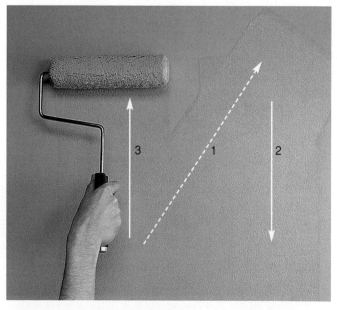

2 Draw the roller straight down (2) from top of the diagonal sweep. Shift the roller to the beginning of the diagonal and roll up (3) to complete the unloading of the roller.

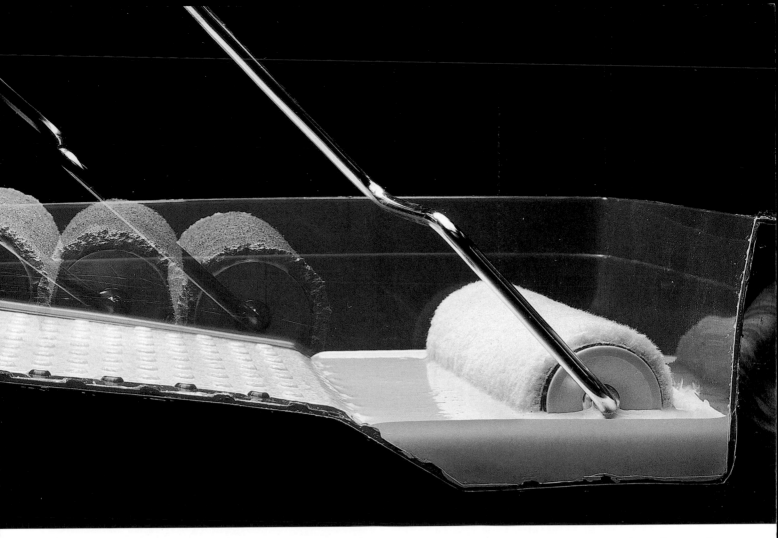

Squeeze out excess liquid. Fill the paint tray reservoir. Dip the roller fully into the reservoir to load it with paint. Lift the roller from the paint reservoir, and roll it back and forth on the textured ramp to distribute the paint evenly onto the nap. The roller should be full, but not dripping, when lifted from the paint pan.

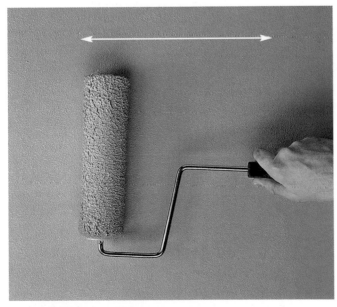

3 Distribute paint over the rest of the section with horizontal back-and-forth strokes.

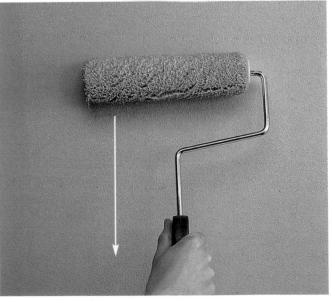

4 Smooth the area by lightly drawing the roller vertically from the top to the bottom of the painted area. Lift the roller and return it to the top of the area after each stroke.

Trim Techniques

When painting an entire room, paint the wood trim first, then paint the walls. Start by painting the inside portions of the trim, and work out toward the walls. On windows, for instance, first paint the edges close to the glass, then paint the surrounding face trim.

Doors should be painted quickly because of the large surface. To avoid lap marks, always paint from dry surfaces back into wet paint. On baseboards, cut in the top edge and work down to the flooring. Plastic floor guards or a wide broadknife can help shield carpet and wood flooring from paint drips.

Alkyds and latex enamels may require two coats. Always sand lightly between coats and wipe with a tack cloth so that the second coat bonds properly.

How to Paint a Window

1 To paint double-hung windows, remove them from their frames if possible. Newer, spring-mounted windows are released by pushing against the frame (see arrow).

2 Drill holes and insert two 2" nails into the legs of a wooden step ladder. Mount the window easel-style for easy painting. Or, lay the window flat on a bench or sawhorses. Do not paint the sides or bottom of the window sashes.

3 Using a tapered sash brush, begin by painting the wood next to the glass. Use the narrow edge of the brush, and overlap the paint onto the glass to create a weatherseal.

4 Remove excess paint from the glass with a putty knife wrapped in a clean cloth. Rewrap the knife often so that you always wipe with clean fabric. Overlap paint from the sash onto the glass by 1/16."

Case molding

Sash

Sill

Apron

5 Paint all flat portions of the sashes, then the case moldings, sill, and apron. Use slow brush strokes, and avoid getting paint between the sash and the frame.

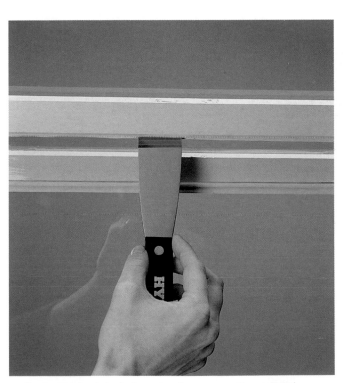

6 If you must paint windows in place, move the painted windows up and down several times during the drying period to keep them from sticking. Use a putty knife to avoid touching the painted surfaces.

How to Paint Doors

1 Remove the door by driving out the lower hinge pin with a screwdriver and hammer. Have a helper hold the door in place. Then, drive out the middle and upper hinge pins.

2 Place the door flat on sawhorses for painting. On paneled doors, paint in the following order, using a brush rather than a roller: 1) recessed panels, 2) horizontal rails, and 3) vertical stiles.

3 Let the painted door dry. If a second coat of paint is needed, sand the first coat lightly and wipe the door with tack cloth before repainting.

4 Seal the unpainted edges of the door with a clear wood sealer to prevent moisture from entering the wood. Water can cause wood to warp and swell.

Tips for Painting Trim

Protect wall and floor surfaces with a wide wallboard knife or a plastic shielding tool.

Wipe all of the paint off of the wallboard knife or shielding tool each time it is moved.

Paint both sides of cabinet doors. This provides an even moisture seal and prevents warping.

Paint deep patterned surfaces with a stiff-bristled brush, like this stenciling brush. Use small circular strokes to penetrate recesses.

Ceiling & Wall Techniques

For a smooth finish on large wall and ceiling areas, paint in small sections. First use a paintbrush to cut in the edges, then immediately roll the section before moving on. If brushed edges dry before the area is rolled, lap marks will be visible on the finished wall. Working in natural light makes it easier to spot missed areas.

Choose high-quality paint and tools and work with a full brush or roller to avoid lap marks and to ensure full coverage. Roll slowly to minimize splattering.

Tips for Painting Ceilings & Walls

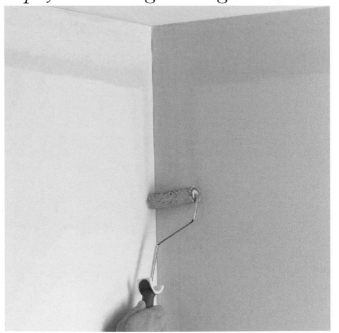

Paint to a wet edge. Cut in the edges on small sections with a paintbrush, then immediately roll the section. (Using a corner roller makes it unnecessary to cut in inside corners.) With two painters, have one cut in with a brush while the other rolls the large areas.

Minimize brush marks. Slide the roller cover slightly off of the roller cage when rolling near wall corners or a ceiling line. Brushed areas dry to a different finish than rolled paint.

How to Paint Ceilings

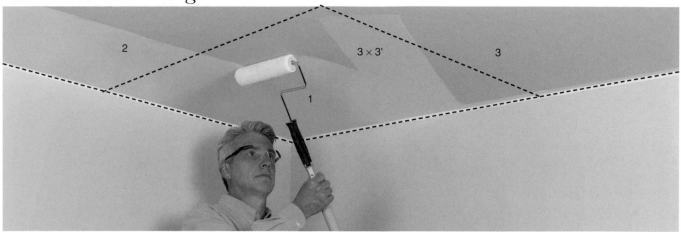

Paint ceilings with a roller handle extension. Use eye protection while painting overhead. Start at the corner farthest from the entry door. Paint the ceiling along the narrow end in 3 × 3' sections, cutting in the edges with a brush before rolling. Apply the paint with a diagonal stroke. Distribute the paint evenly with back-and-forth strokes. For the final smoothing strokes, roll each section toward the wall containing the entry door, lifting the roller at the end of each sweep.

How to Paint Walls

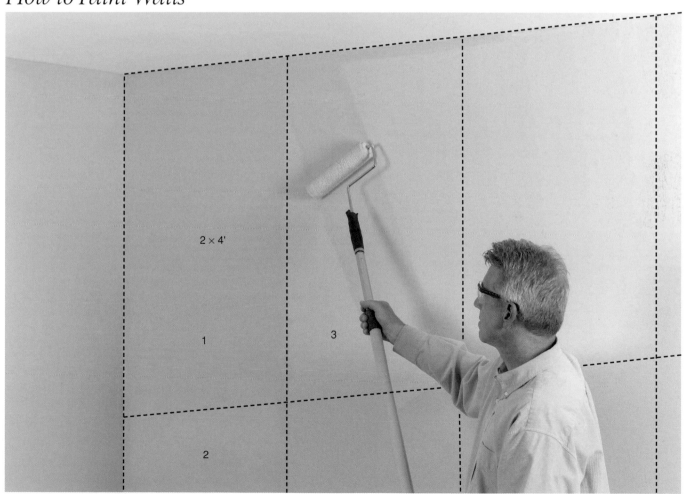

Paint walls in 2 × 4' sections. Start in an upper corner, cutting in the ceiling and wall corners with a brush, then rolling the section. Make the initial diagonal roller stroke from the bottom of the section upward, to avoid dripping paint. Distribute the paint evenly with horizontal strokes, then finish with downward sweeps of the roller. Next, cut in and roll the section directly underneath. Continue with adjacent areas, cutting in and rolling the top sections before the bottom sections. Roll all finish strokes toward the floor.

Texture Painting

*T*exture paints offer a decorating alternative to either flat paints or wallcoverings. The variety of possible effects you can achieve is limited only by your imagination. Texture paints are available in either premixed latex formulations or in dry powder form. Premixed latex texture paints are fine for producing light stipple patterns, but powder textures are a better choice for creating heavier adobe or stucco finishes. Powder textures are available in 25-lb. bags and must be mixed with water, using a paint mixer bit and power drill.

Practice texturing on cardboard until you get the pattern you want. Remember that the depth of the texture depends on the stiffness of the texture paint, the amount applied to the surface, and the type of tool used to create the texture.

How to Texture Paint

Create a swirl pattern with a whisk broom. Apply the texture paint with a roller, then use the broom to create the design.

Use a long-nap roller to make this stipple texture effect. For different patterns, vary the pressure on the roller and amount of texture paint on the surface.

Trowel texture material onto the surface, and pile the material in ridges to create an adobe pattern.

Dab, drag, or swirl a sponge through texture paint to create an endless variety of texture patterns. Or, let the first course dry, then sponge another color on top for a two-tone stucco effect.

Create a crowsfoot design by applying texture paint with a roller, brushing it out level, then randomly striking the surface with the flat side of the brush.

Press the flat side of a trowel into texture paint and pull it away to create a stomp design.

Trowel over a texture pattern when the paint has partially dried, to flatten peaks and achieve a brocade design. Clean the trowel between strokes with a wet brush or sponge.

Cleanup

*A*t the end of a paint job you may choose to throw away the roller covers, but the paint pans, roller handles, and brushes can be cleaned and stored for future use. Stray paint drips can be wiped away if they are still wet. A putty knife or razor will remove many dried paint spots on hardwood or glass. Remove stubborn paint from most surfaces with a chemical cleaner.

Use a spinner tool to remove paint and solvent. Wash the roller cover or brush with solvent, then attach it to the spinner. Pumping the handle throws liquids out of the roller cover or brush. Hold the spinner inside a cardboard box or 5-gallon bucket to catch paint and avoid splatters.

Cleaning products include (from left): chemical cleaner, spinner tool, cleaner tool for brushes and roller covers.

Cleanup Tips

Comb brush bristles with the spiked side of a cleaner tool. This aligns the bristles so they dry properly.

Scrape paint from a roller cover with the curved side of cleaner tool. Remove as much paint as possible before washing the tools with solvent.

Store brushes in their original wrappers, or fold the bristles inside brown wrapping paper. Store washed roller covers on end to avoid flattening the nap.

Remove dried splatters with a chemical cleaner. Before using cleaner, test an inconspicuous area to make sure the surface is colorfast.

Finishing & Refinishing Techniques

*F*inishing or refinishing woodwork or furniture It may seem mysterious and complicated, but even a beginner can produce professional-quality results with surprisingly little mess and fuss when they use the right tools and techniques.

This section shows how to bring new life to woodwork and furniture. It walks you through the process: evaluate the old finish (if there is one); make minor repairs; remove old finishes; sand and fill the wood grain; color and topcoat the wood.

Wastes produced by the stripping and finishing processes may contain lead, mercury, and other dangerous substances that must be disposed of responsibly. If you're not sure about how to do this, contact your local waste management officials or the Environmental Protection Agency for guidelines.

Install fans in windows in your work area to provide ventilation. Where possible, direct one fan outside to remove vapors, and direct another fan into the room to supply fresh air.

Finishing Safety

*P*rotect yourself and your home and help ensure good results by using sensible safety, cleanup, and disposal methods when refinishing. Finishing and refinishing wood can create many hazards, including dangerous vapors, flammable or toxic chemical residue, and sanding dust that can impair breathing (as well as ruin an otherwise good finish).

Make sure you have the necessary safety equipment before you begin working. Organize and ventilate your work area. If you are unsure about disposal regulations, contact your local waste management department or the Environmental Protection Agency (EPA).

Guidelines for a Refinishing Work Area

- Protect the floor with a drop cloth. For messy jobs, lay old newspaper over the drop cloth for easy cleanup.

- Cover any ductwork in the work area to keep dust and fumes from spreading throughout the house.

- Keep the work area well lit, dry, and warm (between 65° and 75°F). To speed drying times, use a dehumidifier in damp areas.

- Extinguish nearby pilot lights and do not operate space heaters when working with strippers and other chemicals that produce flammable vapors.

- Store hazardous or flammable materials in a fireproof cabinet.

- Store knives, scrapers, and other dangerous tools in a locked cabinet or trunk.

- Put the trash in a metal trash can with a lid, and empty it regularly.

Read product labels for important information on safety, cleanup, and disposal.

Safety Equipment

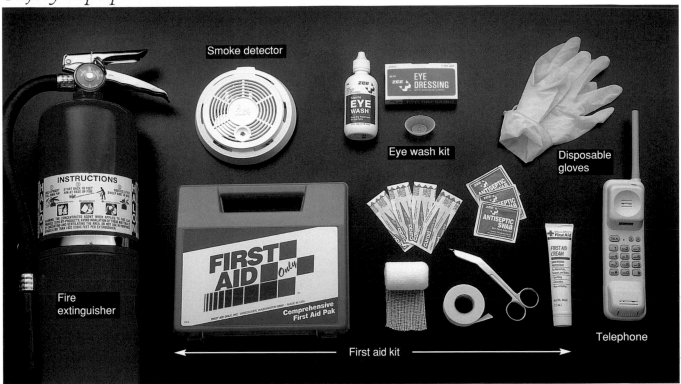

Basic safety equipment for the work area includes: a fully charged fire extinguisher rated for type A and B fires, a smoke detector, a first aid kit, an eye wash kit, disposable latex gloves, and a telephone for emergency use.

Protective Equipment

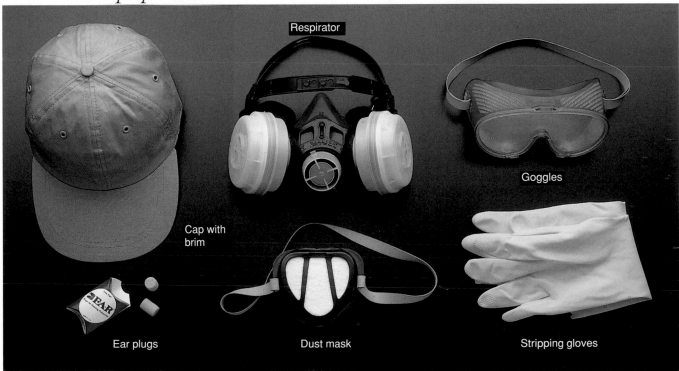

Protective equipment for refinishing and cleanup includes: a dust mask and cap with brim, to wear when sanding; a respirator, to wear when using harsh stripping chemicals; goggles and stripping gloves, to wear while stripping and finishing; ear plugs, to wear when operating power tools.

Removing hardware and other accessories from painted furniture and woodwork can provide useful information about the old finish and the type and condition of the wood.

Evaluation & Planning

Evaluation is a very important step in any refinishing project. Some projects simply are not worth the time, money, and energy required to refinish them. There are, however, signs that indicate good potential and others that should be considered warnings.

When evaluating woodwork or furnishings, find out what type of wood is involved and check out its condition and the condition of its finish.

When evaluating finished woodwork, check for intricate trim pieces and detailed architectural millwork, particularly around doors and windows. Stripping an old finish from detailed woodwork can be very time consuming and physically demanding.

Before deciding to refinish a piece of furniture, look for clues to help establish the value of the piece. If you suspect the piece is antique, have it appraised by a professional before you alter it in any way. (Removing the finish on an antique can significantly reduce its value.) Removing hardware, such as handles, knobs, or hinges, sometimes provides a look at the original finish and lets you determine the type and condition of the wood.

Tips for Evaluating Woodwork for Refinishing

If the woodwork is painted, remove one piece and check the back side to identify the wood type. Also examine the ends of the piece to see how thick the paint is and how deeply it has penetrated into the wood. You may even want to strip the piece to assess how easily the finish comes off. Also, if the piece was easy to remove, consider removing all the woodwork for refinishing, which is easier than refinishing it in place.

Test the condition of the wood. Probe the wood with a sharp instrument, such as an awl, especially around windows and in other areas where moisture could be present. Replace badly rotted woodwork. Minor damage can be treated with wood-hardening products, but this generally means the wood must be painted. Some manufacturers have introduced stainable wood hardeners—check with your local home center.

Tips for Evaluating Furniture for Refinishing

Look at the back or interior of the piece. The type of wood has a great impact on its value and potential as a refinishing project. If the piece is, as the one shown here, made of hardwood, the chances of reviving it are good.

Evaluate the condition of the wood's surface. If the piece has only a few problems, such as small dents and cracks or small burns, it has good potential. However, too many such flaws add to the time required for the project and reduce the probability of its success.

Evaluate the condition of the finish. Some finish blemishes, such as water rings, can be resolved without stripping the old finish. Others require full removal. Also, dark stains usually are absorbed deep into the wood, so if your goal is to create a very light finish, extensive sanding will be required.

Shown cutaway for clarity

Sanding ridge

Clean stained woodwork before you decide to refinish it. A good scrubbing may restore the vitality of the finish enough to satisfy you. If not, you're one step closer to completion of the refinishing project.

Test the old finish with solvents to identify the topcoat material. Dip a clean rag in the solvent you are testing, dab it onto the finish, then look for finish residue on the rag (make sure to give the chemical enough time to work). Always wipe the surface lightly with mineral spirits first to remove any wax buildup.

Identification of Old Finishes

Identifying the original topcoat material is an important stage in both the evaluation and the planning processes. It helps you estimate how much work is involved in removing the topcoat. Knowing the type of topcoat also helps determine your options for restoring the workpiece—some finishes are easier to repair than others, and depending on what you find, you may be able to get by with minor touch-ups and cleaning. Identifying an old finish can suggest the age of a potential project as well (see next page).

To identify a finish, begin by looking for visual clues, like crazing or alligatoring (see next page, step 1). If you are still unsure of the finish material based on this inspection, try dabbing the finish with various solvents. For example, if denatured alcohol dissolves the old topcoat, the chances are good that it's shellac. And once you know it is shellac, you also know that you have the option of blending out surface problems with a mixture of alcohol and shellac.

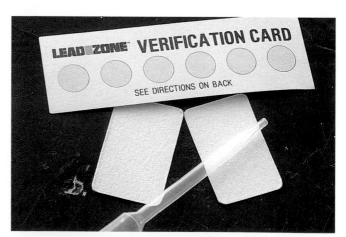

Use a lead-testing kit to determine if paint contains lead. A closely regulated health hazard, lead can be found in paint made before 1978 and was common in paint made before 1950. Follow the kit manufacturer's directions carefully, making sure you test all layers of the finish, not merely the top one. If lead is detected, do not strip or sand the paint yourself. Take it to a professional refinisher.

How to Identify an Old Finish

Oil finish:
- has a natural look, often with a flat sheen, but can be polished to high gloss
- frequently tinted with stain that penetrates deep into the wood
- mineral spirits will dissolve oil, but color must be sanded out
- easy to touch up or recoat

Lacquer:
- very hard finish with a reflective quality; often sprayed on; common on production finishes
- brittle; will craze or fracture (left), especially when exposed to extreme cold
- chips easily
- dissolves and rehardens if treated with lacquer thinner

Shellac:
- alligators and turns dark and gummy as it ages (left)
- usually has an orange cast when dissolved
- very common before 1930, but still in use today
- dissolves easily with denatured alcohol
- will bond with fresh shellac to form a solid topcoat

Varnish / polyurethane:
- most newer varnish products contain polyurethane and are fully dissolved only by strong chemical strippers
- often yellows with age (left)
- common on refinished wood
- polyurethane products cannot be recoated or repaired, but pure varnish may be recoated

1 Look for visual clues to the identity of the topcoat material. Different topcoats exhibit different properties as they age and are subjected to wear and exposure to air and chemicals.

Mineral spirits:
- dissolves wax, most oil topcoats, and pure varnish
- good as a general cleaner
- will lighten some oil-based wood stains

Lacquer thinner:
- dissolves spray-on and brush-on lacquer topcoats
- can be used to repair a lacquer finish
- also dissolves shellac and wax
- a more volatile solvent than mineral spirits or alcohol

Denatured alcohol:
- dissolves shellac on contact
- evaporates quickly; must be wiped off soon after application when used as a finish solvent
- also effective on wax and as a general cleaner

Chemical stripper:
- the most powerful finish-removal agent; cuts through varnish and polyurethane
- different brands are made for different finish materials— check the label
- hazardous chemical; use with care

2 Test with solvents to confirm the identity of the finish. If visual inspection has not given you any clues, test the finish, working from the mildest solvent to the strongest: mineral spirits, then denatured alcohol, then lacquer thinner, then chemical stripper. To test, dab a little solvent onto a clean rag, then rub the rag on the finish, preferably in an inconspicuous area. Allow time for the solvent to work, then rub again, checking to see if any finish residue comes up on the rag. If none of the solvents dissolve the finish, it is probably a commercial topcoat, and sanding is the only effective removal method.

Finish Selection

A good finish protects and beautifies wood. To achieve both goals, a finish is made up of several layers, each with its own specific purpose. Each element should be chosen according to the characteristics of the wood, the function of the piece, and your tastes.

On new wood, apply a seal coat made of sanding sealer to help the finish and color absorb evenly and consistently. For a fine finish, it's better to treat some woods with grain filler instead of sealer.

The next layer is the color layer, which usually is created with wood stain or penetrating oil (pages 137 to 138). Color can either enhance or minimize grain pattern and other wood features, and it can beautify plain wood. (On fine woods or rustic pieces, the color layer can be omitted.)

Finally, a topcoat is applied to seal the wood and protect the finished surfaces from scratches and wear. Topcoats can be created with finishing products such as tung oil and polyurethane. A coat or two of well-buffed paste wax can be applied over most topcoat materials to create a protective surface that is easily renewed with fresh wax.

When selecting a new finish, consider the type of piece you're finishing. If the piece will be used by children or as a food preparation surface, use non-toxic, water-based products to finish the wood.

Tips for Selecting a New Finish

Natural wood

Wood with stain applied

Red oak

Pine

Maple

Consider absorption rates. Some wood types absorb more finish materials than others, depending on the porosity of the grain. In the photo above, the same stain was applied to three different unsealed woods, resulting in three very different levels of darkness. Sealing the wood with sanding sealer or filling the grain first minimizes this effect.

Consider the grain pattern when choosing a finish. Highly figured wood, such as the walnut shown above, usually is given a clear finish so the grain is not obscured. In some cases, tinted penetrating oil can be used to enhance an already striking grain pattern. Experiment with different coloring agents on a piece of similar wood or in an inconspicuous area of the piece.

Sample Finishes: Dark

Use dark finishes to: enhance a distinctive grain pattern (A); add interest to plain wood (B); give a rich, formal look to softwoods (C); create a traditional finish style (D); or simulate the appearance of a finer hardwood on inexpensive wood (E).

Sample Finishes: Light

Use light finishes to: highlight subtle grain patterns (A); amplify attractive wood tones (B); modify wood tones to match a particular decor or color scheme (C); add a sense of depth (D); or give unfinished wood a seasoned, antique appearance (E).

Finishing Tools

*F*or any refinishing project, you will need a few hand and power tools to remove the old finish, repair defects and damage, prepare the workpiece for the new finish, and apply the new finish. You probably already own many of the necessary tools, especially the more basic ones (see list right). Some household items, such as old toothbrushes and cotton swabs, can also be useful in refinishing and finishing. Other household items can be fashioned into custom finish-removal tools. For example, an old credit card, cut to fit the contours, can be used as a molding scraper.

TOOLS & MATERIALS

- Brad pusher
- Clamps
- Craft knife
- Dust mask
- Eye protection
- Hammer
- Nailset
- Razor-blade scraper
- Respirator
- Rubber gloves
- Rubber mallet
- Screwdrivers
- Staple gun
- Straightedge
- Tape measure
- Utility knife
- Wood chisels
- Drop cloths
- Masking tape

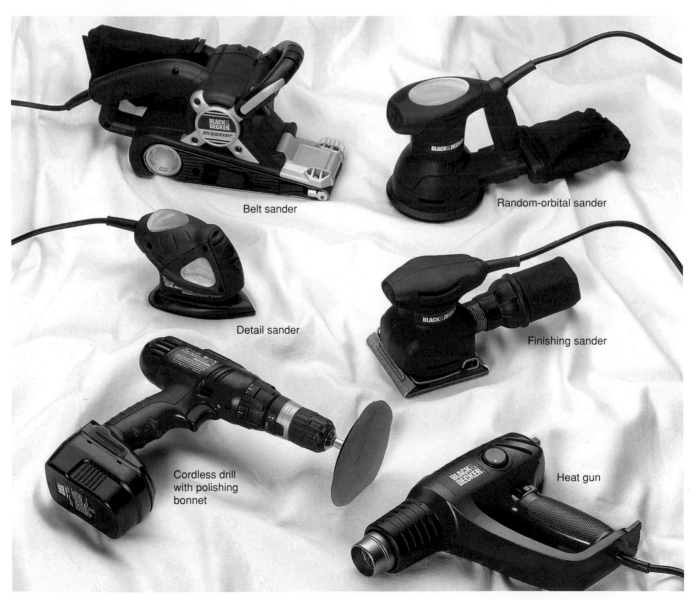

Belt sander

Random-orbital sander

Detail sander

Finishing sander

Cordless drill with polishing bonnet

Heat gun

Power tools for finishing and refinishing include a belt sander for finish removal on large, flat surfaces; a random-orbital sander for all-purpose sanding; finishing sanders for early stages of finish sanding, a cordless drill with a polishing bonnet for buffing topcoats; a heat gun for stripping paint; and a mouse-sander for detail sanding.

Brushes for removing finish include a stripping brush and wire brush for finish removal, and wire detail brushes for smaller areas. Brushes for applying finish include a painting pad for large, flat areas; a polyester-bristle brush for all finishes; a natural-bristle brush for oil-based applications; artists' brushes for touch-ups; stenciling brushes for finishing and liquid wax applications.

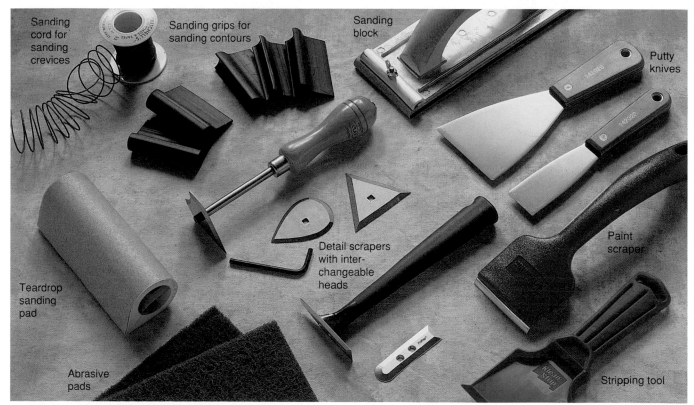

Sanding and scraping tools include: a stripping tool, paint scraper, and putty knives for finish removal and scraping flat surfaces; detail scrapers for scraping detail areas; a sanding sponge for all flat surfaces; abrasive pads and synthetic steel wool for finish removal, sanding, and buffing finishing coats; sanding cord, sanding grips, and a teardrop sanding pad for sanding hard-to-reach areas and contours.

Finish Removal

Removing an old finish does not have to be tedious. In fact, watching a project emerge from beneath an old finish is one of the most satisfying stages of the process. Nevertheless, stripping a finish should be viewed as a last resort to be done only if the old finish cannot be saved.

Before beginning the removal process, make certain the project really needs stripping. Clean the wood surfaces thoroughly and identify the finish topcoat to make sure it can be repaired (pages 120 through 123).

There are three primary finish-removal methods: scraping and sanding, heat stripping, and chemical stripping. Removing a finish usually requires a combination of techniques. Scraping and sanding are done at the beginning and end of almost every finish-removal process. Sanding is the only way to remove some very stubborn finishes, such as epoxy paint. Heat stripping is most effective with painted finishes, but it can be used with some success on thick layers of clear topcoat. In most cases, heat stripping should be followed by chemical stripping.

Chemical stripping is the most thorough finish-removal method. It removes nearly any finish, and it is the only effective removal method for polyurethane products.

Tip:

When refinishing furniture, remove the hardware whenever possible. When it's not possible to remove the hardware or accessories, mask them carefully.

Scraping & Sanding

*B*efore using heat or chemicals to strip wood, scrape off loose finish with a paint scraper or putty knife. After stripping, use scrapers again to dislodge any remaining flecks. Finally, sand to remove any finish residue and smooth the surface of the wood.

Scraping and sanding are the primary method for removing tough finishes, such as epoxy paint, and for delicate surfaces that cannot be stripped with heat or chemicals.

Choose a sander or other tool suited to the size and shape of the area to be sanded. (Never use a belt sander on fine furniture.) Always sand with the grain of the wood.

Successful heat stripping depends on good timing. As you expose paint to a heat gun, the paint reaches a point where its bond with the wood loosens. If you scrape the surface at this point, the scraper works like a plow, pushing the loosened paint off the wood in wide ribbons. If you wait too long, the paint becomes gummy.

Heat Stripping

Using heat to strip an old finish is safe and effective as long as you use the proper techniques and safety measures. It works best on paint but also can be used on thick layers of varnish, lacquer, and other topcoats. Even if you plan to use a chemical stripper, you may want to heat-strip the wood first—you'll use less of the chemical stripper if you do. Scrape off loose paint before using a heat gun on painted woodwork.

TOOLS & MATERIALS

- Heat gun
- Putty knife
- Assorted scrapers
- Heavy-gauge extension cord
- Fire extinguisher
- Coffee can
- Goggles
- Work gloves
- Aluminum foil
- Cardboard

Tip for Heat-stripping

A heat shield keeps the heat gun from damaging or blistering the finish on surrounding areas. For a shield, use a piece of sheet metal or cover-heavy cardboard with heavy-duty aluminum foil.

How to Heat-strip Paint

1 Scrape off all loose paint flakes, using a paint scraper. Hold the heat gun about 2" above the surface, and then turn it on, starting at the lowest setting. Move the gun in a circular motion until the paint begins to blister. If the paint doesn't blister, try the next higher heat setting.

2 Follow the heat gun with a metal scraper. Hold the scraper at about a 30° angle, and move both the scraper and the heat gun at the same speed. (Always move the heat gun in a circular motion.) Strip all the large, flat surfaces. Deposit the ribbons of paint in a coffee can or other heat-proof container.

3 Heat-strip the contoured and uneven areas, using specialty scrapers, where needed, to remove the loosened paint. Do not overheat or use too much pressure around detailed areas— they are more vulnerable to scorching and gouging than flat areas.

4 Dry-scrape all wood surfaces to remove any remaining loosened paint flecks after you are done heat stripping. In most cases, you will need to use chemical solvents or strippers to remove the rest of the finish.

Finishing & Refinishing Techniques 131

Chemical Stripping

Chemical solvents are fast and thorough. They can remove just about any finish material, from varnish to polyurethane or paint. Before choosing a solvent or stripper, identify the old finish type. Remember that most finishes are composed of several layers and try to select a chemical that is effective on the materials in all the layers (pages 122 to 123).

The primary solvents used for stripping are mineral spirits, denatured alcohol, and lacquer thinner. These chemicals are inexpensive and relatively safe, so use them instead of commercial strippers whenever possible.

Commercial strippers are strong chemicals that dissolve just about any finish. For most jobs, a semi-paste stripper is the best choice. Unlike liquid stripper, it clings to most surfaces and will not dry out before the finish is dissolved. There is quite a range of semi-paste strippers to choose from. By reading the labels, you will find that most are created for specific finish types. There are varnish removers paint removers, and even polyurethane removers.

In the past, strippers almost always contained hazardous chemicals, requiring you to wear a respirator and other protective equipment. These strippers are still common, and they are very effective. For most refinishing projects, other strippers are better choices. New products without hazardous chemicals dissolve most finishes with far less risk, although they work somewhat slower than the more hazardous varieties.

TOOLS & MATERIALS

- Paintbrushes
- Putty knife
- Assorted scrapers
- Safety equipment
- Stripper or solvent
- Medium abrasive pads
- Newspapers and rags
- Sawdust
- Rinsing agent

Chemical stripper dissolves thick finishes so they can be wiped off or scraped off easily. Coarse abrasive pads are effective removal tools for contours.

How to Chemically Strip a Finish

1 Pour some stripper into a small, easy-to-use container (no more than you can use in 15 minutes). Read the label and select a brush for applying the stripper—most brands can be applied with inexpensive polyester-bristle brushes.

2 Wearing rubbers gloves (and a respirator if the label advises you to use one), apply a thick coat of stripper to the work-piece, beginning at the top of the project and working down from there. Do not overbrush the stripper.

3 Let the stripper work for the length of time suggested by the manufacturer. Remove the sludge with a putty knife or strip-ping knife, and deposit it on old newspapers. TIP: Just before you start to scrape away the sludge, sprinkle sawdust on the stripper to make it easier to remove.

4 Strip the detailed and contoured areas, using specialty scrapers and abrasive pads to remove the sludge. Use light pressure on the scrapers so you do not gouge the wood.

5 Apply a thin coat of stripper to the wood, and then scrub off any remaining finish, using a synthetic-bristle stripping brush or medium abrasive pads.

6 Clean the wood with a medium abrasive pad dipped in the rinsing agent recommended by the stripper manufacturer (of-ten denatured alcohol). This removes most traces of the finish and the stripper.

Surface Preparation

Surface preparation ensures an even, high-quality finish. Finish sand with progressively finer grits of sandpaper, starting with 150-grit. Generally, hardwood requires finer-grit sandpaper than soft wood. To speed up the process, use a power sander for the first stages of the sanding, then switch to hand-sanding to complete the process.

Finish sanding alone creates a smooth surface, but because wood absorbs stain at different rates, the color can be blotchy and dark. Sealing wood with sanding sealer evens out the stain-absorption rates and yields a lighter, more even finish. Filling the grain creates a finish that feels as smooth as it looks.

With grain filler

With sanding sealer

Finish-sanded only

Use sanding sealer or grain filler for a fine finish. Finish sanding alone (left) can leave a blotchy surface, but sanding sealer (center) plus grain-filler (right) give progressively finer finishes.

Tips on Using Sanding Sealer

Make your own sanding sealer by blending one part clear topcoat material (not water-based) with one part topcoat solvent. NOTE: Use the same topcoat material you plan to apply to the project.

Wipe on a heavy coat of the sealer, then wipe off the excess after a few minutes. When dry, sand lightly with 220-grit sandpaper.

How to Finish Sand

1 Finish sand all surfaces with 150-grit sandpaper, following the direction of the grain. Use a finishing sander on flat surfaces and specialty sanding blocks on contours. When sanding hardwood, switch to 180-grit paper and sand again.

2 Raise the wood grain by dampening the surface with a wet rag. Let the wood dry, then skim the surface with a fine abrasive pad, following the grain.

3 Use sanding blocks to hand-sand the entire workpiece with the finest-grit paper in the sanding sequence. Sand until all sanding marks are gone and the surface is smooth. (Use bright sidelighting to check your progress.) If using sanding sealer, do that now (see page 134).

How to Apply Grain Filler

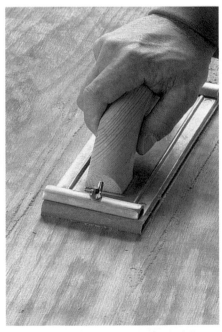

1 After finish sanding, use a rag or putty knife to spread a coat of grain filler onto the wood surface. With a polishing motion, work the filler into the grain. Let the filler dry until it becomes cloudy (usually about 5 minutes).

2 Remove excess filler by drawing a plastic scraper across the grain of the wood at a 45° angle. Let the grain filler dry overnight.

3 Lightly hand-sand the surface, following the direction of the grain, with 320-grit sandpaper. Finally, dampen a clean cloth with mineral spirits and use it to thoroughly clean the surface.

A well-chosen, properly applied color layer is the most important component of an attractive wood finish.

Color Application

The most common reason for coloring wood is to enhance its appearance by showing off a fine or distinctive grain pattern creating a beautiful wood tone. Stain and penetrating oil, the two most basic coloring agents, also accomplish more practical results: dark colors conceal uneven coloration and can blend different wood types.

When selecting a coloring agent, consider oil-based stain, water-based stains, wipe-on gel stains, penetrating oils, and one-step stain-and-sealant products, among others. To sort through the many options, start by finding a color you like, and then read the label to determine if it's the best product for your project. Make sure it will work with the topcoat you plan to use.

On any product, carefully read and follow the manufacturer's directions. Drying times, application techniques, and cleanup methods vary widely between products. Test the product on a wood sample or on an inconspicuous area of the project, and keep a careful record of what you used and how many coats you applied.

After stripping, some wood is discolored, and evening out the color with dark stain is easier than trying to sand out the discolorations. Because stain forms a more opaque color layer than penetrating oil, it's generally a better product for covering wood problems.

How to Use Penetrating Oil

1 Prepare for the stain (pages 134-135), then apply a heavy coat of penetrating oil to all surfaces, using a staining cloth. Wait 15 to 30 minutes, recoating any areas that begin to dry out. Apply oil to all surfaces, and let it soak into the wood for 30 to 60 minutes.

2 Wipe the surface dry with a clean cloth, rubbing with the wood grain. Apply another coat of oil with a clean cloth, then let the oil dry overnight. NOTE: Two coats are sufficient in most cases, since further coats will not darken the finish color.

3 Dab a few drops of penetrating oil onto a fine abrasive pad, then rub the surfaces until smooth. Let the oil dry for at least 72 hours before applying a topcoat. If you do not plan to topcoat the finish, buff with a soft cloth to harden the oil finish.

How to Apply Liquid Stain

1 Stir the stain thoroughly and apply a heavy coat with a brush or cloth. Stir the stain often as you work. Let the stain soak in according to manufacturer's instructions.

2 Remove the excess stain with a clean, lint-free cloth. Wipe against the grain first, then with the grain. If the color is too dark, try scrubbing the surface with water or mineral spirits. Let the stain dry, then buff the surface with a fine abrasive pad.

3 Apply light coats of stain until the desired color is achieved. Buff between coats and after the final coat before adding the topcoat.

How to Apply Gel Stain

1 Stir the stain, then work it into the surfaces of the workpiece with a staining cloth, rubbing in a circular motion. Recoat any areas that dry out as you work, and cover as much of the workpiece as possible.

2 Use a stiff-bristled brush, such as a stencil brush, to apply the gel in hard-to-reach areas.

3 Let the stain soak in according to manufacturer's directions, then wipe off the excess with a clean rag, using a polishing motion. Buff the stained surface with the wood grain, using a soft, clean cloth.

4 Apply additional coats until the desired color has been achieved. (Most manufacturers recommend at least three coats.) Let the stain dry, then buff the workpiece with a fine abrasive pad.

Topcoat Application

opcoats seal the wood, protect the finish from scratches and other wear, and increase the appearance of the wood. Because they dry clear, topcoats highlight the coloring and natural figure of the wood. For most projects, a topcoat of tung oil, polyurethane, or paste wax will protect the wood and give it the appearance you want.

When choosing a topcoat, consider durability, sheen, and compatibility with the coloring agents you have or want to use. Other factors, such as drying time, ease of application and cleanup, and safety, should also influence your choice.

Some one-step stain-and-seal products are also available. Test these products on scrap wood or an inconspicuous area of the project before working on the visible surfaces of the project.

Protect your finish and wood with a topcoat layer, like the wipe-on tung oil being applied to this dresser.

How to Apply Tung Oil

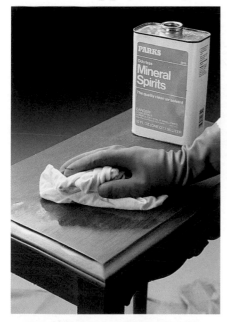

1 Clean the surfaces thoroughly with a cloth and mineral spirits. Apply a thick coat of tung oil with a cloth or brush. Let the tung oil penetrate for 5 to 10 minutes, then rub off the excess with a cloth, using a polishing motion.

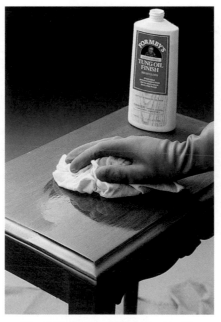

2 After 24 hours, buff the tung oil with a clean cloth, and then reapply additional coats as necessary to build the finish. (Three coats are generally considered the minimum for a good finish.) Use a clean cloth to apply each coat.

3 Let the finish dry completely, then buff it lightly with a fine abrasive pad. For a higher gloss, buff the surface with a polishing bonnet and a cordless drill.

How to Apply Polyurethane

1 Seal unstained wood with a 1:1 mixture of polyurethane and a thinning agent, such as water or mineral spirits (check the product label). Apply the sealer with a clean cloth or brush and let it dry. Wipe off excess sealer, using a clean cloth. NOTE: Wood that has been colored with stain or penetrating oil does not need a seal coat.

2 Apply a coat of polyurethane, starting at the top of the project and working your way down. When the surface is covered, smooth out the finish by lightly brushing in one direction only, parallel to the grain. Let dry, then sand the surface with 600-grit wet/dry sandpaper.

3 Apply the second coat. To keep the finish from running, always try to position the workpiece so the surface being top-coated is horizontal.

4 OPTION: After the final coat dries, wet-sand the surface with a fine abrasive pad to remove any small imperfections and diminish the gloss.

How to Apply Paste Wax

1 Apply a moderate layer of paste wax to the wood, using a fine abrasive pad or a cloth. Rub the wax into the wood with a polishing motion.

2 Allow the wax to dry until it becomes filmy in spots. Gently wipe off any exess, undried wax, and then allow the remaining wax to dry until filmy (usually within 10 to 20 minutes). NOTE: Do not let the wax dry too long or it will harden and become very difficult to buff.

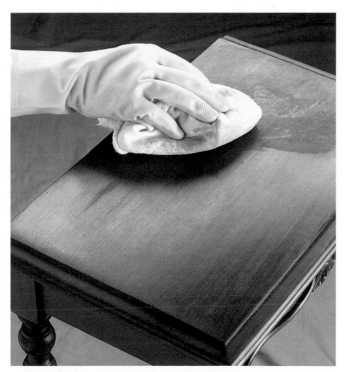

3 Begin buffing the wax with a soft cloth, using a light, circular motion. Buff the entire surface until the filminess disappears and the wax is clear.

4 Continue buffing the wax until the surface is hard and shiny. Apply and buff another coat, then let the wax dry for at least 24 hours before applying additional coats. Apply at least three coats for a fine wax finish.

Wallcovering Techniques

Wallcovering can be the single most important element in a decorating scheme, setting the style of the room and gracefully pulling together the chosen color scheme. Although many people joke about the difficulty of applying wallcovering, with the right tools, materials, and techniques, two people can paper a room as well as a professional.

This section will walk you through the wallcovering process, from selecting the most appropriate type of wallcovering, to hanging the product on walls and ceilings. There are also easy-to-follow charts that simplify the task of measuring and estimating for wallcovering.

The following pages contain numerous professional tips that will improve your efficiency and help you achieve flawless results. For instance, you will learn how to create a hanging plan and mark the walls before you begin hanging strips. The hanging plan makes easy work of matching patterns, making sure seams line up with corners, and positioning partial strips in inconspicuous areas.

When you are ready to begin wallcovering, the step-by-step instructions will show you how to prepare the strips and hang them on walls or ceilings. You will also find methods for wallcovering around corners, doors, windows, pipes, radiators, fixtures, and even archways. There are also techniques for hanging wallcovering borders and panels.

Wallcovering Selection

*V*ery few modern "wallpapers" are actually made of paper. Today's wallcoverings may be made of vinyl, vinyl-coated paper or cloth, textiles, natural grasses, foil, or mylar. Vinyl or coated vinyl coverings are the easiest to hang, clean, and remove. Other types of wallcoverings can give a room a unique look but may require special handling. Your choice of wallcovering depends on the needs of the room and on your confidence and ability with wallcovering.

Types of Wallcovering

Vinyl wallcoverings are made with a continuous flexible film, often applied over a fabric or paper backing. Some vinyls successfully duplicate the effect of natural grasscloth or textile wallcoverings. Vinyl wallcoverings with preapplied adhesives are a good choice because they are easy to apply, clean, and remove.

Foils or mylars are coated with a thin, flexible metallic film. These highly reflective wallcoverings add brightness to a room, but they require careful handling. Foils also reveal all wall flaws, so surface preparation must be perfect.

Grasscloths are imported wallcoverings that use natural plant fibers. Because they reflect little light, grasscloths soften the appearance of a room. They are a good choice for flawed, irregular walls. Hang them with clear adhesive. Never use water to rinse grasscloths.

Fabric wallcoverings are made of woven textiles. Fabrics are easy to hang because there is no pattern to match, but they may be difficult to clean.

Embossed wallcoverings are stamped with a relief pattern for an elegant, formal appearance. Never use a seam roller on embossed wallcoverings: they can be easily damaged.

Tips for Choosing Wallcovering

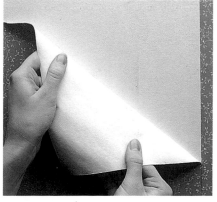

Removability: Strippable wallcoverings (left) can be pulled away from the wall by hand, leaving little or no film or residue. Peelable wallcoverings (right) can be removed but may leave a thin paper layer on the wall, which can usually be removed with soap and water. Check the back of the sample or the wallcovering package for its strippability rating. Choose a strippable product to make future redecorating easier.

Washability: Washable wallcoverings can be cleaned with mild soap and water and a sponge. Scrubbable wallcoverings are durable enough to be scrubbed with a soft brush. Choose scrubbable wallcoverings for heavy-use areas.

Application: Prepasted wallcoverings (left) are factory-coated with water-base adhesive that is activated when wallcovering is wetted in a water tray. Unpasted wallcoverings (right) must be coated with an adhesive for hanging. As well as being easier to prepare, prepasted products are just as durable as those requiring an adhesive coat.

Dye-lot: Jot down dye-lot numbers for reference. If you need additional rolls, order from the same dye-lot to avoid slight color differences.

Packaging: Wallcoverings are sold in continuous triple, double, and single-roll bolts.

Patterns: There is always more waste with large patterns. A wallcovering with a large drop pattern can be more expensive to hang than one with a smaller repeat. With large designs, it may also be difficult to avoid pattern interruptions at baseboards or corners.

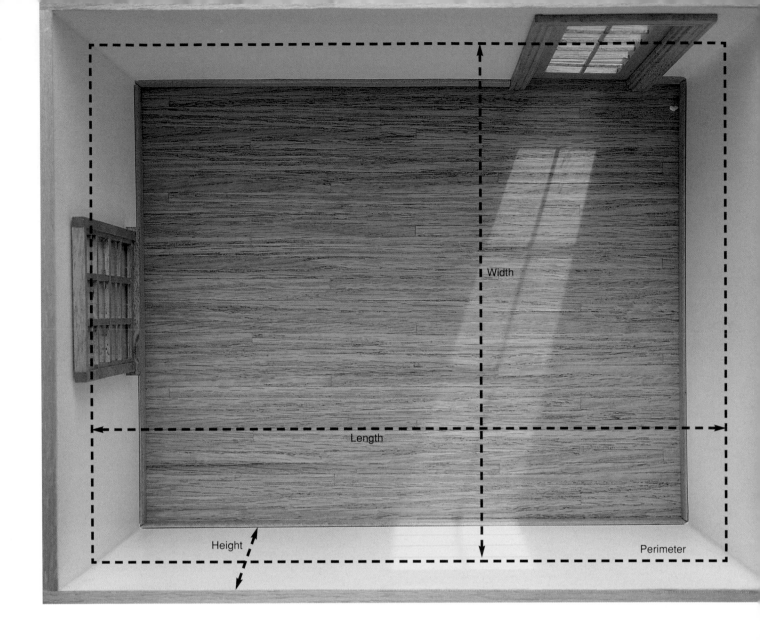

Width

Length

Height

Perimeter

Measuring & Estimating Methods

With a few room measurements and the information listed on the wallcovering package, you can estimate the correct amount of wallcovering to buy. The procedure given on these two pages will help you calculate the square footage of your walls and ceilings and show you how to find the per-roll coverage of wallcovering.

Because of normal trimming waste, the actual per-roll coverage of wallcovering will be at least 15% less than the coverage listed on the package. The waste percentage can be higher depending on how much space it takes for the wallcovering pattern to repeat itself. This "pattern repeat" measurement is listed on the wallcovering package. You can compensate for this extra waste factor by adding the pattern repeat measurement to the wall height measurement of the room.

Measure the room:

Walls: Measure the *length* of the wall, to the nearest ½ ft. (Add the length of all the walls to find the perimeter if the entire room will be wallcovered.) Include window and door openings in wall measurements. Measure the *height* of surfaces to be covered, to the nearest ½ ft. Do not include baseboards or crown moldings in height measurement. **Ceilings:** Measure the length and the *width* of ceiling to the nearest ½ ft.

How to Measure Unusual Surfaces

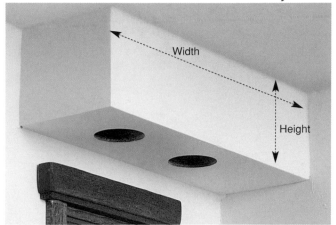

Soffits: If you are covering the sides of a soffit, add the width and height of each side into the wall measurement.

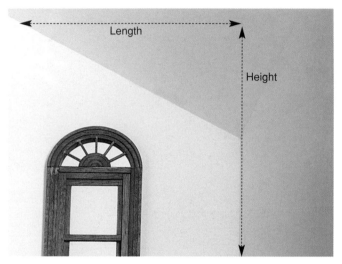

Triangular walls: Measure as though the surface is square: length × height.

Wallcovering packages or pattern books give per-roll coverage, in square feet, and the drop pattern repeat measurement.

How to Figure Actual Per-roll Coverage

1) Total per-roll coverage (square feet)	
2) Adjust for waste factor	× .85
3) **Actual per-roll coverage** (square feet)	=

How to Calculate Rolls Needed for a Ceiling

1) Room length (feet)	
2) Wallcovering pattern repeat (feet)	+
3) Adjusted length (feet)	=
4) Room width (feet)	×
5) Ceiling area (square feet)	=
6) Actual per-roll coverage (figured above; square feet)	÷
7) **Number of rolls needed for ceiling**	=

How to Calculate Rolls Needed for Walls

1) Wall height (feet)	
2) Wallcovering pattern repeat (feet)	+
3) Adjusted height (feet)	=
4) Wall length; or room perimeter (feet)	×
5) Wall area (square feet)	=
6) Actual per-roll coverage (figured above; square feet)	÷
7) Number of rolls	=
8) Add 1 roll for each archway or recessed window	+
9) **Number of rolls needed for walls**	=

Paint pail

Natural sponge

Laser level

Water tray

Bubblestick

Paint tray & roller

Smoothing brushes

Smoothing tool

Wallboard knife

Seam roller

Razor knife

Wallcovering scissors

Tools

Many of the tools for hanging wallcovering are common items you may already own. Keep a supply of #2 pencils and a pencil sharpener handy for precise marking when laying out and cutting wallcovering. Never use an ink marker or ballpoint pen, because the ink might bleed through the wet wallcovering.

Use a bubblestick or carpenter's level for establishing plumb lines and as a straightedge for cutting. Don't use a chalk line: the chalk can smear the new wallcovering or ooze through the seams. Trim wallcoverings with a razor knife that features breakaway tips. Buy noncorrosive paint pails for holding wash water, and use a natural or high-quality plastic sponge to avoid damaging the wallcovering.

Wallcovering adhesives can be applied with an ordinary paint roller, but you will need a smoothing tool to flatten the wallcovering strips as you hang them, and a seam roller to fix the joints between strips. Ask your dealer about the proper tools for your wallcovering.

Smoothing brushes come in various nap lengths. Use a short nap brush for smoothing out vinyl wallcoverings. A soft, long nap brush is used for fragile wallcoverings, like grasscloths.

A razor knife with breakaway blades is used for trimming wallcovering at ceilings, baseboards, corners, windows, and doors. Renew tips often to avoid snagging and tearing the wallcovering.

Use a wide broadknife to hold wallcoverings tightly while trimming overlaps in corners and against window or door casings. A narrower broadknife may work better for intricate corners.

(continued next page)

Wallcovering Tools *(continued)*

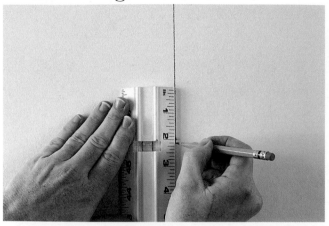

A bubblestick or carpenter's level is used to mark verticals for a plumb line, and doubles as a straightedge for cutting. Use a level instead of a chalk line: chalk can bleed through wallcovering seams.

Use wallcovering scissors to trim wallcovering at the seam where wall and ceiling coverings meet. A razor knife may puncture the underlying ceiling strip.

A wallcoverer's table provides a flat working surface. Wallcovering stores lend or rent tables. Or, you can make your own by placing a sheet of plywood on sawhorses.

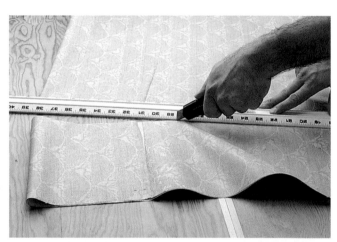

Hold a straightedge tightly against the booked wallcovering strip and cut with a sharp razor knife to form partial strips for corners. Hold the knife blade straight while cutting the strip.

A wallcovering tray holds water for wetting prepasted wallcovering strips.

A sponge and bucket are used for rinsing down strips. Use a natural or quality synthetic sponge.

Use a paint roller or paste brush to apply adhesive to the backs of unpasted wallcovering strips.

Materials

Before hanging wallcovering, the wall surfaces must be both sealed and sized to prevent the adhesives from soaking into the wall surface. Today's premixed primer-sealers do both jobs with a single application.

If your wallcovering is not pre-pasted, you will need one or more types of adhesive. For most vinyl or vinyl-backed wallcoverings, choose a heavy-duty premixed vinyl adhesive that contains a mildew inhibitor. Vinyl wallcoverings also require a special vinyl-on-vinyl adhesive for areas where the wallcovering strips overlap, such as around wall corners and archways.

When hanging specialty wallcoverings, you may need special adhesives. Natural grasscloths, for instance, require a clear-drying adhesive that will not soak through and stain the fibers. Check the wallcovering label or ask your dealer about the correct adhesive for your application.

Latex primer-sealers seal and size walls in one application. These are available as a powder or in premixed form. Heavy-duty vinyl adhesive is used to hang vinyl or vinyl-backed wall-coverings. Vinyl-on-vinyl adhesive fastens lap seams on vinyl wallcoverings. It is also used to apply vinyl borders over vinyl wallcoverings.

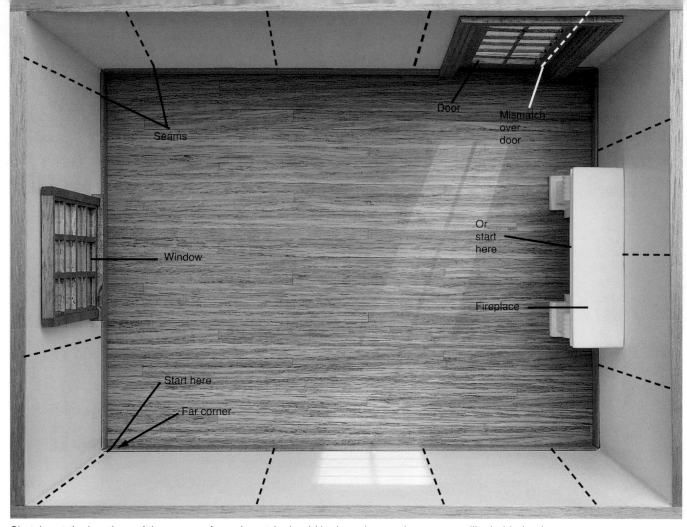

Sketch out the locations of the seams. Any mismatch should be in an inconspicuous area, like behind a door.

The Hanging Plan

Tips for Planning Seams

Plan the mismatch. If the room has no obvious focal point, start at the corner farthest from the entry. Measure out a distance equal to the wallcovering width and mark a point. Work in both directions, marking out points where the seams will fall.

When hanging any patterned wallcovering, there will be one seam where a full strip meets a partial strip. The pattern will usually mismatch at this point. Plan this mismatched seam in an inconspicuous spot, like behind a door or above an entrance.

Sketch out seam lines before you begin. Avoid placing seams that will be difficult to handle. A seam that falls close to the edge of a window or fireplace complicates the job. At corners, wallcovering should always overlap slightly onto the opposite wall. If one or more seams falls in a bad spot, adjust your plumb line a few inches to compensate.

Start at a focal point, like a fireplace or large window. Center a plumb line on the focal point, then sketch a wall covering plan in both directions from the center line.

Adjust your plan for corners that fall exactly on seam lines. Make sure you have at least ½" overlap on inside corners, and 1" on outside corners.

Adjust for seams that fall in difficult locations, like near the edges of windows or doors. Shift your starting point so that the seams leave you with workable widths of wallcovering around these obstacles.

Plan a ceiling layout so that any pattern interruption will be along the least conspicuous side of the room. Pattern interruptions occur on the last ceiling strip, so begin hanging covering opposite the side where the room is entered.

Reroll each wallcovering roll with the pattern side in. Inspect the pattern surface for color and design flaws. Return any flawed rolls to your dealer.

Wallcovering Handling Techniques

For durability and easy application, choose a quality prepasted vinyl wallcovering whenever possible. Clear the room of all furniture that can be easily removed, and layer newspapers or drop cloths next to the walls. For easy handling, rent a wallcoverer's table, or make your own (page 150).

Shut off the electricity to the room at the main service panel, and check all switches and outlet receptacles to be sure the power is off. Remove the receptacle and switch coverplates. Cover the receptacle slots with masking tape to keep out water and adhesive.

For the best visibility and drying conditions, work during the daylight hours. And have another person help you whenever possible. A helper is especially useful when covering ceilings.

As you hang the wallcovering, make sure each strip is perfectly positioned before going on to the next. You can adjust the strips once they are on the wall, but make the initial placement carefully, as too much adjusting can stretch some coverings and may wrinkle and tear.

Tip:
Some premium wallcoverings have unprinted side edges (called "selvages") that protect the roll. The selvages must be cut off the wallcovering strip with a razor knife and straightedge before hanging. The selvages may have printed guide marks for precise cutting.

How to Measure & Cut Wallcovering Strips

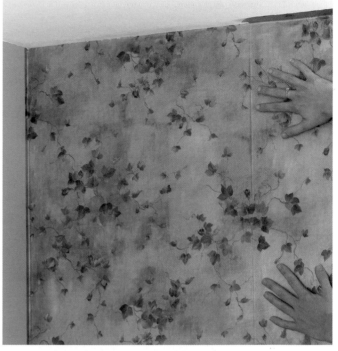

1 Hold the wallcovering strip against the wall. Make sure there is a full pattern at the ceiling line and that the strip overlaps the ceiling and baseboard by about 2". Cut the strip to length with scissors.

2 For the next strips, find the pattern match with the previously hung strip. Then, measure and cut the new strip with about 2" of excess at each end.

How to Handle Prepasted Wallcovering

How to Handle Unpasted Wallcovering

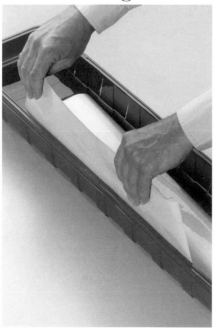

1 Fill a water tray half full of lukewarm water. Roll the cut strip loosely with the pattern side in. Soak the roll in the tray as directed by the manufacturer, usually about 1 minute.

2 Holding one edge of the strip with both hands, lift the wallcovering from the water. Watch the pasted side to make sure the strip is evenly wetted. Book the strip as indicated (page 156).

Lay the strip with the pattern side down on a wallcoverer's table or flat surface. Apply adhesive evenly to the strip, using a paint roller. Wipe any adhesive from the table before preparing the next strip.

How to Book Wallcovering Strips

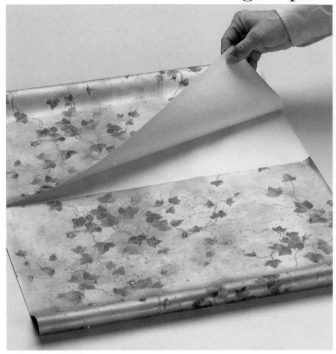

"Book" wallcovering by folding both ends of the strip into the center, with the pasted side in. Do not crease the folds. Let the strip stand (cure) for about 10 minutes. Some wallcoverings should not be booked: follow the manufacturer's directions.

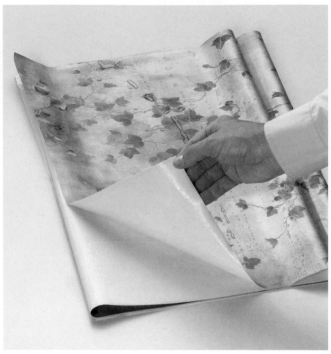

For ceiling strips or wallcovering borders, use an "accordion" book. Fold the strip back and forth with the pasted side in for easy handling. Let the strip stand (cure) for about 10 minutes.

How to Position & Smooth Wallcovering

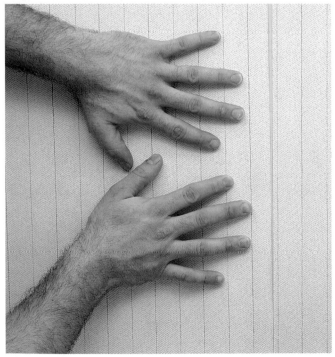

1 Unfold the booked strip and position it lightly with its edge butted against a plumb line or previous strip. Use flat palms to slide the strip precisely into place. Flatten the top of the strip with a smoothing brush.

2 Beginning at the top, smooth the wallcovering out from the center in both directions. Check for bubbles, and make sure the seams are properly butted. Pull the strip away and reposition it if necessary.

How to Trim Wallcovering

1 Position a 10" or 12" drywall knife along the cut, then cut along the edge with a sharp utility knife. Keep the utility knife blade in place while changing the position of the drywall knife.

2 With wallcovered ceilings, crease the wall strips with the drywall knife, then cut along the crease with scissors. Cutting with a utility knife may puncture the ceiling strip.

How to Roll Seams

Let the strips stand for about ½ hour. Then, roll the seam gently with a seam roller. Do not press out the adhesive by rolling too much or too forcefully. Do not roll seams on foils, fabrics, or embossed wallcoverings. Instead, tap the seams gently with a smoothing brush.

How to Rinse Wallcovering

Use clear water and a sponge to rinse adhesive from the surface. Change the water after every three or four strips. Do not let water run along the seams. Do not use water on grasscloths, embossed wallcoverings, or fabrics.

Ceiling & Wall Techniques

Wallcovering a ceiling is easier if you have another person to help you. Let your helper hold one end of the accordion-folded strips as you place the other end.

Dust your hands with talcum powder when handling dry wallcovering, to avoid smudges. When planning a ceiling job, remember that the pattern on the last wallcovering strip may be broken by the ceiling line. Since the least visible ceiling edge is usually on the entry wall, begin hanging ceiling strips at the far end of the room, and work back toward the entryway.

If you plan to cover the walls as well as the ceiling, remember that the ceiling pattern can blend perfectly into only one wall. Plan the ceiling job so the strips will blend into your chosen "match" wall.

How to Wallcover a Ceiling

1 Measure the width of the wallcovering strip and subtract ½". Near a corner, measure this distance away from the wall at several points, and mark points on the ceiling with a pencil.

2 Using the marks as guides, draw a guide line along the length of the ceiling with a pencil and straightedge. Cut and prepare the first wallcovering strip (page 155).

3 Working in small sections, position the strip against the guide line. Overlap the side wall by ½", and the end wall by 2". Flatten the strip with the smoothing brush as you work. Trim each strip after it is smoothed.

4 Cut out a small wedge of wallcovering in the corner so that the strip will lie flat. Press the wallcovering into the corner with a wallboard knife.

5 If the end walls will also be covered, trim the ceiling overlap to ½". Leave a ½" overlap on all walls that will be covered with matching wallcovering.

On walls that will not be covered, trim the excess by holding a wallboard knife against the corner and cutting with a sharp razor knife. Continue hanging strips, butting the edges so that the pattern matches.

How to Wallcover Walls

1 From your starting point, measure a distance equal to the width of the wallpaper minus ½" and mark a point. At that point, draw a vertical plumb line from the ceiling to the floor, using a bubblestick or level.

2 Cut and prepare the first strip (page 155). Unfold the top portion of the booked strip and position it against the plumb line so the strip extends beyond the ceiling joint by about 2".

3 At the corner foldline, snip the top of the strip so the wallcovering wraps around the corner without wrinkling. Using your open palms, slide the strip into position, with the edge butted against the plumb line. Smooth the strip with a smoothing brush.

4 Unfold the bottom of the strip. Use your open palms to position it against the plumb line. Smooth the strip with a smoothing brush, carefully pressing out any bubbles.

5 Trim the excess wallcovering at the ceiling and baseboard, using a drywall knife and a sharp utility knife. With clean water and a sponge, rinse any adhesive from the surface of the wallcovering.

6 Hang additional strips, sliding strips into place so the pattern matches exactly. Let the strips stand for about half an hour, then roll the seams lightly with a seam roller. (On embossed or fabric wallcoverings, gently tap the seams with a smoothing brush.)

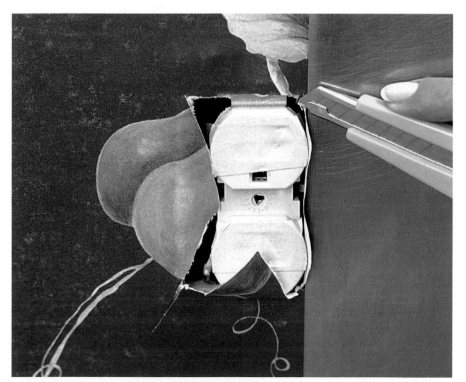

7 Hang wallcovering over receptacle and switch boxes, then use a utility knife to make small diagonal cuts to expose the box. Finally, trim the paper to the edges of the box. NOTE: Turn off the power to the circuit and remove coverplates before beginning the project.

Tip:

When applying the first strip, make sure there is a full pattern at the ceiling line. Also, when applying wallcovering to walls that meet a ceiling with wallcovering, mark the plumb line at the starting point straight down from a ceiling seam.

How to Wallcover Around an Inside Corner

1 Cut and prepare a full strip. While the strip cures, measure from the edge of the preceding strip to the corner at several points, then add ½" to the longest of these measurements. Align the edges of the booked strip. From two points, measure a distance equal to the measurement made in Step 1. Hold a straightedge against the marked points and cut the strip, using a sharp utility knife.

2 Position strip, carefully butting the edges so pattern matches exactly and the wallcovering overlaps the ceiling by about 2" and the next wall by about ½".

3 Make corner slits at the top and bottom of the strip to wrap the overlap around the corner without wrinkles. Flatten the strip with a smoothing brush, the trim the excess at the ceiling and baseboard.

4 Measure the remainder of the strip you cut in Step 1, and mark a point equal to this measurement. At this mark, draw a plumb line from the ceiling to the floor on the new wall.

5 Position the strip on the wall with the cut edge in the corner and the leading (uncut) edge against the plumb line drawn in Step 4. Press the strip flat with a smoothing brush. Trim the excess at the ceiling and baseboard.

6 If you are using vinyl wallcovering, peel back the edge and apply vinyl-on-vinyl adhesive to the lap seam. Press the seam area flat. Let the strips stand for about 30 minutes, then roll the seams and rinse the area with a damp sponge.

Variation: Outside corners usually can be covered by wrapping the strip around the edge without cutting it. If the corner is not plumb, follow the directions for inside corners, except add 1" to the Step 1 measurement to allow for a wider wrap.

Window & Door Techniques

Do not try to precut wall-covering strips to fit the shape of windows or doors. Hang a full strip right over the casing, then smooth the strip before trimming the edges along the door or window. Make diagonal cuts to fit the wallcovering around sharp corners. To avoid damaging the wood on these diagonal cuts, use scissors instead of a razor knife.

If short strips are hung directly above and below an opening, make sure they are hung exactly vertical to ensure a good pattern fit with the next full strip. Do not trim the short strips until the last full strip has been hung. This allows for small adjustments in case of slight mismatches.

How to Wallcover Around Windows & Doors

1 Position the strip on the wall, running over the window casing. Butt the seam against the edge of the previous strip.

2 Smooth the flat areas of wallcovering with a smoothing brush. Press the strip tightly against casing.

3 Use scissors to cut diagonally from the edge of the strip to the corner of the casing. Make a similar cut in the bottom corner if you are wallcovering around a window.

4 Use scissors to trim away excess wallcovering to about 1" around the inside of the frame. Smooth the wallcovering and press out any bubbles as you work.

5 Hold the wallcovering against the casing with a wallboard knife, and trim excess with a sharp razor knife. Trim overlaps at the ceiling and baseboard. Rinse the wallcovering and casings, using a damp sponge.

6 Cut short strips for sections above and below the window. You may find scraps that will match the pattern and fit these spaces. Hang small strips exactly vertical to ensure a pattern match with the next full strip.

(continued next page)

7 Cut and prepare the next full strip. Position it on the wall with its edge butting the previous strip so that the pattern matches.

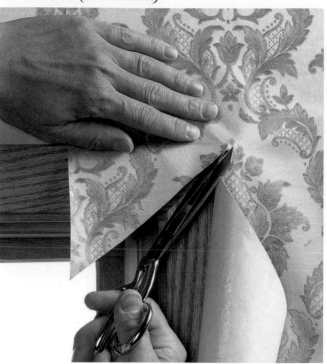

8 Snip the top and bottom corners diagonally from the edge of the strip to the corners of the casing. Trim away excess wallcovering to about 1" around the inside of the window or door frame.

9 Match the seam on the bottom half of the strip. Trim the excess wallcovering to about 1" with scissors. Flatten the strip with a smoothing brush.

10 Hold the wallcovering against the casing with a wallboard knife, and cut the excess with a sharp razor knife. Trim the overlaps at the ceiling and baseboard. Rinse the wallcovering and casings, using a damp sponge.

How to Wallcover a Recessed Window

1 Hang the wallcovering strips so they overlap the recess. Smooth the strips and trim the excess at the baseboard and ceiling. To wrap the top and bottom of the recess, make a horizontal cut at the halfway point to within ½" of the wall.

2 From the horizontal cut (Step 1), make vertical cuts to the top and bottom of the recess. Make small diagonal cuts to the corners of the recess.

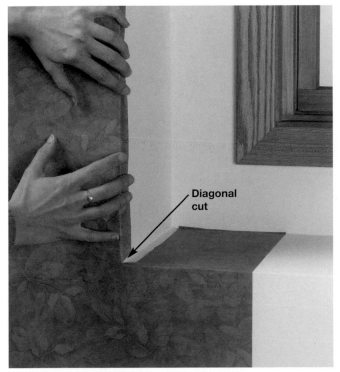

Diagonal cut

3 Fold the upper and lower flaps of the wallcovering onto the recessed surfaces. Smooth the strips and trim them at the back edge. Wrap the vertical edge around the corner. Hang wallcovering around the window if needed (pages 166).

4 Measure, cut, and prepare a matching piece of wallcovering to cover the side of the recess. The side piece should slightly overlap the top and bottom of the recess and the wrapped vertical edge. Use vinyl-on-vinyl adhesive to glue the overlapped seams.

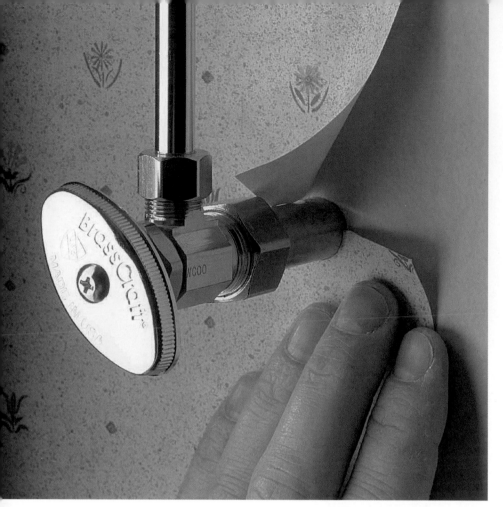

Pipe, Radiator, & Fixture Techniques

Hanging wallcovering around sinks, pipes, and other obstacles requires cutting into wallcovering strips. Hold the strip so that patterns match, and cut from the edge closest to the fixture. If possible, cut along a pattern line to hide the slit. At the end of the slit, cut an opening to fit around the fixture. With wall-mounted sinks, tuck small wallcovering overlaps behind the sink.

How to Wallcover Around a Pipe

1 Pull out the escutcheon from the wall. Hold the wallcovering strip against the wall so that the pattern matches the previous strip. From the closest edge of the strip, cut the slit to reach the pipe.

2 Press the strip flat up to the pipe with a smoothing brush.

3 Cut a hole at the end of the slit to fit around the pipe. Butt the edges of the slit together and brush them smooth.

How to Wallcover Around a Wall-mounted Sink

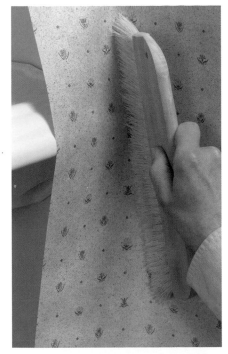

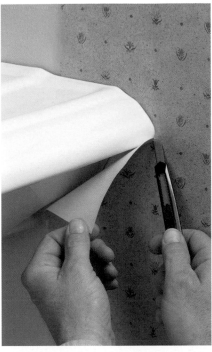

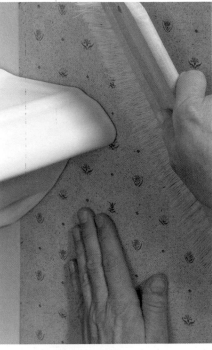

1 Brush the wallcovering strip up to the edge of the sink. Cut horizontal slits in the wallcovering, leaving a ¼" overlap at the top and bottom of the sink.

2 Trim the wallcovering around the side of the sink, leaving a slight overlap.

3 Smooth the wallcovering. Tuck the excess wallcovering into the crack between the sink and the wall if possible, or trim the overlap.

How to Wallcover Behind a Radiator

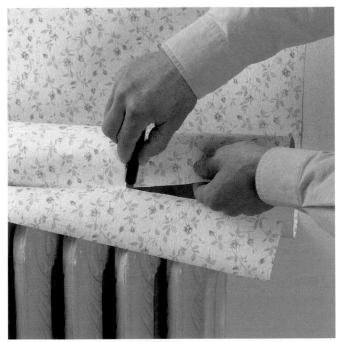

1 Unfold the entire strip and position it on the wall. Smooth the strip from the ceiling to the top of the radiator. Use a flat wooden yardstick to smooth the strip down behind the radiator. Crease the wallcovering along the baseboard with the yardstick.

2 Pull the bottom of the strip up from behind the radiator. Trim the excess wallcovering along the crease line. Smooth the covering back down behind radiator with the yardstick.

How To Wallcover an Archway

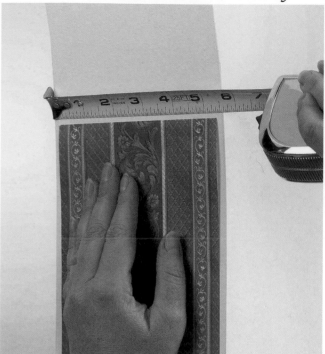

1 Some wallcoverings are available with matching borders that can be used to cover the inside of an archway. Or, measure the inside of the archway and cut the strip from standard wallcovering. The strip should be ¼" narrower than the inside surface of archway.

Archway Techniques

Cover the inside surface of an archway with wallcovering after the walls are finished. Wrap the wall strips around the edges of the archway, then hang a matching strip or wallcovering border around the inside surface to cover the wrapped edges. Make a series of small slits in the wall strips along the archway curve so that the wallcovering lies smoothly. Use vinyl-on-vinyl adhesive to hang the archway strip.

2 Hang the wallcovering on both sides of the archway, with the strips overlapping the archway opening. Smooth the strips and trim the excess at the ceiling and baseboards.

3 Use scissors to trim the overlapping wallcovering, leaving about 1" of excess.

4 Make small slits in the wallcovering along the curved portion of the archway, cutting as close as possible to the wall edge.

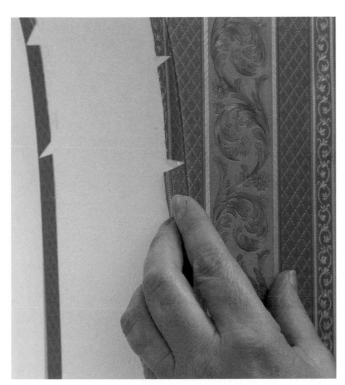

5 Wrap the cut edges inside the archway and press them flat. If the adjacent room will be wallcovered, wrap the wallcovering around the edge of the archway from both sides.

6 Coat the back of the archway strip with vinyl-on-vinyl adhesive. Position the strip along the inside of the archway with a ⅛" space on each edge of the strip. Smooth the strip with a smoothing brush. Rinse the strip, using a damp sponge.

Wallcovering Borders

Wallcovering borders are available in a variety of designs, and you can use them to complement any painted or wallcovered wall. Hang a border as a crown molding around a ceiling, or as a frame around windows, doors, and fireplaces. When using a border to outline or frame features of a room, select a border with a nondirectional print, as a directional print may be less appealing when hung upside down.

When hanging borders, start in an inconspicuous area, such as the hinge-side of an entry door. This is important because a mismatch usually occurs where the last border segment meets the first. You can run a border in a continuous band around doors and windows using a simple overlapping technique to cut perfect miter joints at the corners.

How to Hang Wallcovering Borders

1 If you are positioning the border somewhere other than along the ceiling or baseboard, create a level line in the desired position. Shoot a line with a laser level or draw a light pencil line around the room, using a carpenter's level. Cut and prepare the first border strip following the methods for preparing unpasted wallcovering (page 155).

2 Begin at the least conspicuous corner, overlapping the border onto the adjacent wall by ½". Have a helper hold the accordion-booked border while you apply it and smooth it with a smoothing brush.

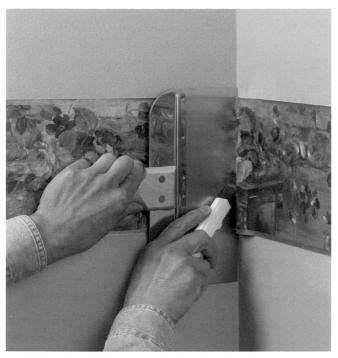

3 At inside corners, create a ¼" tuck from the overhang. Apply the adjoining strip and trim it with a razor knife. Peel back the tucked strip and smooth the strip around the corner, overlapping the border on the adjacent wall. Press the border flat. Apply seam adhesive to the lapped seam, if necessary.

4 Where a seam falls in the middle of a wall, overlap strips so the patterns match. Cut through both layers, using a razor knife and a wallboard knife. Peel back the strips and remove the cut ends. Press the strips flat. Roll the seam after half an hour and rinse with a sponge.

How to Miter Border Corners

1 Apply the horizontal border strip, extending it past the corner a distance greater than the width of the border. Apply the vertical strip over the horizontal one.

2 Hold a straightedge along points where the strips intersect, and cut through both layers. Peel back the strips and remove the cut ends.

3 Press the strips back into place. After half an hour, lightly roll the seam and rinse any adhesive from the area, using a damp sponge.

Panels

By combining wallcovering and coordinating borders, you can create decorative wall panels to add interest and elegance to painted walls. Use the panels to divide large walls into smaller sections, or position them to highlight pictures or mirrors. Make the panels identical in size, or alternate wide panels with narrow ones.

For a balanced appearance, space the panels evenly on the wall, leaving slightly more space below the panel than above. Begin by planning the placement of the most dominant or conspicuous panels first. It may help to sketch the room on graph paper, taking into account the position of windows, doors, and furnishings. Also account for any pattern repeat in the wallcovering to allow for matching patterns.

Before you cut any wallcovering, make false panels from butcher paper and tape them to the walls according to your plan. Once the false panels are in place, use them to draw layout lines for the real panels.

How to Make Wallcovering Panels

1 Determine the size and position of the wallcovering panels by cutting and taping paper to the wall. Using a pencil and a carpenter's level, mark the outline of the panels on the wall. Measure and record the dimensions of each panel.

2 Cut a strip of wallcovering for the center of each panel to size, using a framing square to ensure 90° angles at the corners. Prepare the strip following the instructions on pages 154-156.

3 Unfold the top portion of the booked strip. Press it lightly on the wall, aligning the edges with the marked lines. Use flat palms to slide the strip into place. Press the top of the strip flat with a smoothing brush, and check for bubbles.

4 Unfold the bottom half of the strip. Use flat palms to position the strip against the marked lines. Press the strip flat with a smoothing brush, checking for bubbles.

5 Cut and apply any remaining strips, matching the pattern and butting the seams. Roll the seam after ½ hour. Rinse any adhesive from the wallcovering and wall, using clear water and a damp sponge. Prepare the border, using border adhesive and following the methods for preparing unpasted wallcovering (pages 155-156).

6 Apply the border strips in a clockwise direction, starting at the least conspicuous corner. Butt the inner edges of the border to the panel edges. Miter the corners (page 173). Smooth the first corner only lightly until the final strip is applied. Roll the outer edges of the border and seams after ½ hour.

Finishing Touches

How to Fix a Bubble

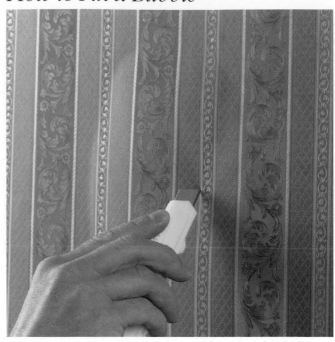

*A*fter you have finished wallcovering a room, check for areas to touch up while the job is still fresh. Pay special attention to the seams: if you rolled the seams too hard, or rolled them before the adhesive set, you may have squeezed too much adhesive from under the edges of the covering. These edges will look tight while they are wet but will bubble after the covering is dry. Reglue the edges of the seam as shown.

Inspect the wallcovering for bubbles, loose spots, and other flaws, using a strong sidelight. Stand close to the wall and look down its length, against the light.

1 Cut a slit through the bubble, using a sharp razor knife. If there is a pattern in the wallcovering, cut along a line in the pattern to hide the slit.

2 Insert the tip of a glue applicator through the slit and apply adhesive sparingly to the wall under the wallcovering.

3 Press the wallcovering gently to rebond it. Use a clean, damp sponge to press the flap down and wipe away excess glue.

How to Patch Wallcovering

1 Fasten a scrap of matching wallcovering over the damaged portion with drafting tape, so that the patterns match.

2 Holding a razor knife blade at a 90° angle to the wall, cut through both layers of wallcovering. If the wallcovering has strong pattern lines, cut along the lines to hide the seams. With less definite patterns, cut irregular lines.

How to Fix a Seam

3 Remove the scrap and patch, then peel away the damaged wallcovering. Apply adhesive to the back of the patch and position it in the hole so that the pattern matches. Rinse the patch area with a damp sponge.

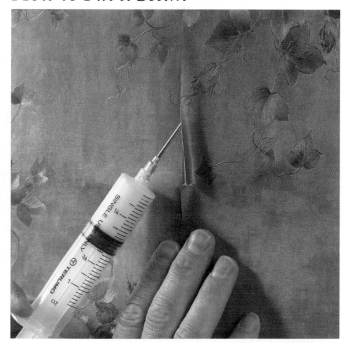

Lift the edge of the wallcovering and insert the tip of a glue applicator under it. Squirt adhesive onto the wall and gently press the seam flat. Let the repair stand for ½ hour, then smooth the seam lightly with a seam roller. Wipe the seam lightly with a damp sponge.

Advanced Painting & Decorating

Advanced Paint Designs & Finishes

Beyond solid colors and plain finishes lies a host of advanced techniques you can use to creatively express yourself through decorating projects. In this section, you will learn to combine modern tools and materials with the time-honored techniques mastered by artists and decorators. With the right tools and a little practice, you can master any of these effects, then use your imagination to expand or adapt the techniques for your own custom finishes.

First, you will learn about the special tools used to create specific effects. You'll learn how to make paint glazes, following given formulas to improve the texture and increase the workability of your paint. From there, it's a simple matter of selecting the design or finish that will add new life to a room or a touch of illusion to a dull surface.

The painting techniques in this section range from simple strip designs to stenciled patterns and metallic finishes. Look through all of the techniques and see how they can be tailored or combined to suit your home and your tastes. For example, you can add depth to the symmetry of stripes by adding a texture or glazed finish.

For best results, prepare the surface (page 60) you will be painting and apply a base coat of paint or primer if necessary. Practice the techniques and try out the colors you've chosen on a large piece of mat board before starting a project.

Advanced Painting Tools

Many tools and paintbrushes have been developed for creating specialized decorative painting effects. Depending on how they are used, some tools may create more than one effect. Working with the various tools and learning their capabilities is an important step in becoming a successful faux finisher. Most tools and paintbrushes are available in a range of sizes. As a general rule, use the largest size tool or brush suitable for the surface area.

Some tools and brushes are designed for manipulating the wet glaze on the surface. These include: floggers (A), blending brushes or softeners (B), stipplers (C), and a mottler (D). Also helpful is a dual Woolie (E) roller and an edging tool (F).

Certain faux effects are achieved using removal tools, such as a wood graining rocker (G), overgrainers (H), wipe-out tools (I), and combs (J). Artist's erasers (K) can be notched and used as combs (page 225). Rag rollers (L) are also available for faux effects.

Specialty brushes designed for applying paints and glazes include artist's brushes, such as rounds (M), liners (N), or a dagger (O). These may be used for veining in marble finishes or graining in wood finishes. Stenciling brushes (P) are available in ¼" to 1¼" diameters. Other tools, such as a sea sponge (Q) or feathers (R) are also used for applying paints and glazes. A check roller (S) is a specialty tool used for applying pore structure in a faux oak finish.

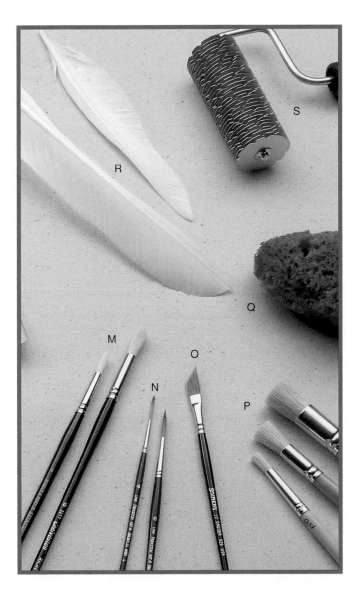

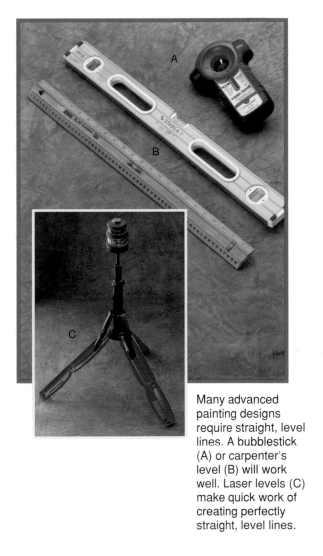

Many advanced painting designs require straight, level lines. A bubblestick (A) or carpenter's level (B) will work well. Laser levels (C) make quick work of creating perfectly straight, level lines.

Advanced Painting Materials

Latex and acrylic paints can be used successfully for a wide range of faux finishes and techniques. Because they are water-based, they are easy to clean up with just soap and water, and they are also safer for the environment than oil-based paints.

Water-based paints dry quickly, which is not necessarily an advantage in decorative painting, especially for techniques that require some manipulation of the paint on the surface. To increase *open time,* or the length of time the paint can be manipulated, several paint additives have been developed. These include latex paint conditioner, such as Floetrol, and acrylic paint extender. These products are available at paint retailers and craft supply stores.

For some decorative painting techniques, it is preferable to use a paint glaze, which is usually thinner and more translucent than paint. There are some premixed acrylic paint glazes available in limited colors. These may be mixed to produce additional glaze colors. Untinted acrylic mediums in gloss, satin, or matte finishes also are available for mixing with acrylic or latex paint to make glazes. The glaze medium does not change the color of the paint; generally a small amount of paint is added to the glaze medium, just enough to give it the desired color. Latex or acrylic paint can also be mixed with water-based urethane or varnish for a very translucent glaze.

Tips for Using Paint Glazes

• Protect the surrounding area with a drop cloth or plastic sheet, and wear old clothing because working with a glaze can be messy.

• Use a wide painter's tape (page 84) to mask off the surrounding surfaces. Firmly rub the edges of the tape to ensure that the glaze will not seep under it.

• Use a paint roller to apply the glaze when even coverage is desired or when painting a large surface, such as a wall.

• Use a paintbrush to apply the glaze when smooth finish is desired, or when painting a small item.

• Use a sponge applicator to apply the glaze when more variation and pattern in the surface is desired, or when painting a small item.

• Manipulate glaze while it is still wet. Although humidity affects the setting time, the glaze can usually be manipulated for a few minutes.

• Work with an assistant when using glaze on a large surface. While one person applies the glaze, the other can manipulate it.

Low-luster latex enamel paint is used for the base coat under faux finishes. The slightly sheened surface gives the finish a base to cling to, while allowing manipulation tools to move easily on the surface.

Acrylic paints are available in a wide range of colors. They can be used alone for stenciling, or mixed with acrylic mediums to create glazes for decorative paint finishes.

Premixed acrylic paint glazes are available in a variety of colors for faux finishing. They are slightly translucent and contain additives for extended open time.

Acrylic mediums, or glaze mediums, can be mixed with acrylic or latex paint to create paint glazes with gloss, satin, or matte finishes.

Advanced Paint Designs & Finishes 185

Two-color Meshing

Dozens of techniques can be used to produce interesting textured surfaces, but most require several steps. With this technique, you can create lovely color variations in only one step. It's quick and easy enough for any beginner.

This technique is designed to be used with satin-finish, standard latex paints—no glazes are necessary. In fact, glazes are not compatible with this technique.

When choosing paint, start by choosing your lightest color, and then find a second color that is three to five shades darker than the first. Colors that are three shades apart produce muted variations, while colors that are five shades apart produce more dramatic textures.

TOOLS & MATERIALS

- Dual roller
- Two-compartment paint tray
- 1-inch brush
- Edging tool
- Masking tape
- Two colors of satin-finish latex paint

How to Apply Meshed Color

1 Select two colors of satin-finish latex paint, one color three-to-five shades darker than the other. Stir the paint well, then pour each color into one compartment of a divided paint tray.

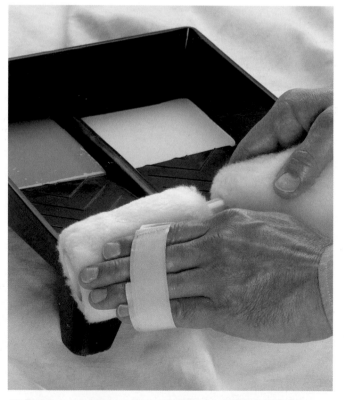

2 Remove any lint from the paint roller by patting it with the sticky side of masking tape. Change the tape when it loses its stickiness, and continue patting until no more lint comes off the roller. Dampen the roller with water and thoroughly wring it out.

3 Roll the two-color roller into the paint and run it up and down the textured portion of the tray several times. Make sure the roller is loaded well, but not so full that it will drip.

4 Make a diagonal sweep about two feet long, rolling slowly enough to avoid splatters. Make a second diagonal sweep in the opposite direction, then a third, sweep vertical.

5 Draw the roller in a back and forth motion until the colors are blended to your satisfaction.

6 At the edges and in corners, apply ample splotches of each paint color, using a 1" brush. Immediately pat the paint with the accessory pad to blend the colors to match the surrounding area.

Taped-off Designs

Simple techniques using painter's masking tape can help you create stripes and geometric designs of all kinds. Select a professional-quality tape that prevents paint seepage and can be removed easily without damaging the base coat. For best results, apply the paint in light coats, but be careful not to thin the paint too much.

Alternating colors produce striking results; so does alternating between flat paint and a gloss finish. Whatever type of design you choose, measure the room and plan the pattern so it works out evenly around the room.

A laser level makes applying tape for the stripes practically foolproof. If you plan on doing a large project or several taped-off designs throughout your home, consider purchasing one.

TOOLS & MATERIALS

- Carpenter's level
- Pencil
- Tape measure
- Small paint roller
- Paintbrush or paint roller, for base coat
- Latex or craft acrylic paints
- Painter's masking tape
- Sponge applicator

How to Paint a Striped Design

1 Apply a base coat in the desired color. Allow the paint to dry completely.

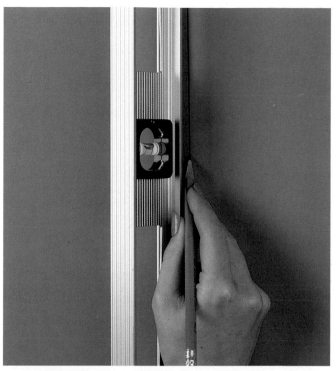

2 Mark light plumb lines for the first stripe, using a pencil and a carpenter's level. Apply painter's masking tape along the lines, and press the edges firmly to ensure a good bond.

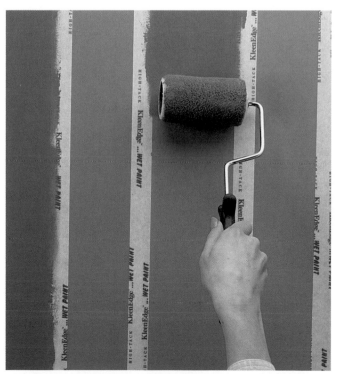

3 Measure from the first stripe, and draw parallel lines for the remaining stripes of the first color. Use the level to plumb each line. Apply the masking tape. Paint the stripes, using a paintbrush, small roller, or sponge applicator. Allow the paint to dry.

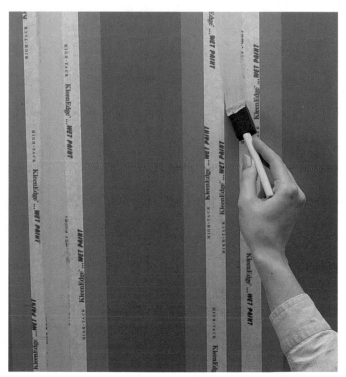

4 Remove the masking tape from the painted stripes. Repeat the process for any additional colors.

How to Apply an Alternating Matte and Gloss Finish

TOOLS & MATERIALS

- Large paintbrush
- 1" paintbrush
- Flat, square artist's brush
- Pencil
- Straightedge
- Laser level or carpenter's level
- Matte latex paint
- High-gloss acrylic varnish

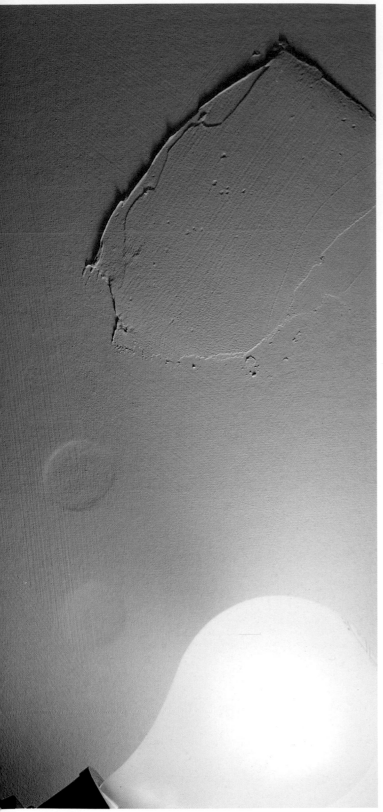

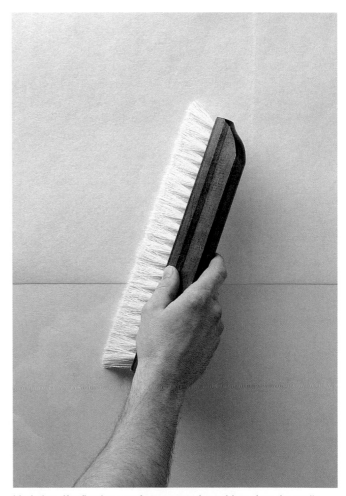

1 Fill all dents and holes, and sand away any bumps or ridges on the walls. (The gloss finish will magnify any surface flaws, so the walls must be perfectly flat and flawless.) Check the surface with a strong sidelight.

Variation: If a flawless surface cannot be achieved on the walls, hang heavy-duty lining paper before starting the project.

2 Apply two coats of matte latex paint over the walls. Let the paint dry according to manufacturer's instructions.

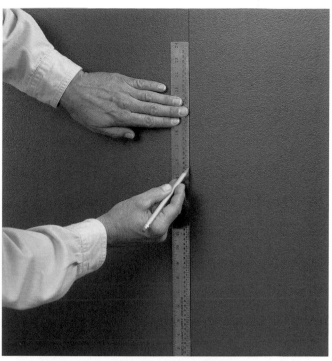

3 Measure walls and plan the design. Divide the height of the room until you find dimensions that will result in full squares at the baseboard and ceiling. Use a laser level or carpenter's level and a straightedge to draw the vertical and then the horizontal lines of the design.

4 Tape off the outline of every other square. Press the edges of the tape to ensure a good bond and seal the edges.

5 Apply a coat of high-gloss varnish within the taped-off squares. Allow the varnish to dry, and then apply a second coat. Remove the tape.

Sponge Painting

Sponge painting produces a soft, mottled effect and is one of the easiest techniques to master. The look of sponge painting is determined by the number of paint colors applied, the sequence in which they are applied, and the distance between the sponge impressions.

The sponge used is crucial. You can use a natural sea sponge, which will produce small, condensed marks, or sculpt a synthetic sponge to create a larger, more defined pattern.

Semigloss, satin, and flat latex paints all are appropriate for sponge painting. For a translucent finish, you can use a paint glaze consisting of paint, paint conditioner, and water (see page 193).

Before starting your project, select the sponge and paint colors, and practice on a piece of mat board or a scrap of drywall until you're satisfied with the effect.

TOOLS & MATERIALS

- Paintbrushes and rollers for base coat
- Roller tray
- Large synthetic sponge
- Latex paint for base coat
- Latex paint in two colors, one light and one dark
- Latex paint conditioner (optional)

How to Sponge Paint

1 Apply a coat of the base color, and let it dry completely.

2 Tear out small chunks from the surface and around the edges of one side of the sponge. Make sure the entire surface is pitted with holes of various depths. Dampen the sponge and squeeze out as much of the water as possible.

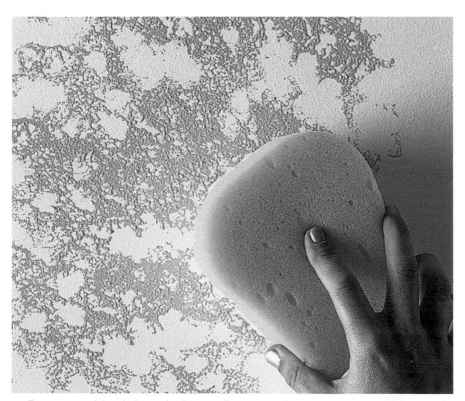

3 Pour some of the darker color into a roller tray, and press the pitted surface of the sponge into the paint. Pat the sponge onto a paper towel to remove the excess paint, and then use it to dab paint onto the wall. (Use a small chunk of the sponge to sponge paint into the corners.)

SPONGING GLAZE

Mix together the following ingredients:
1 part latex or craft acrylic paint
1 part latex paint conditioner
1 part water

(continued next page)

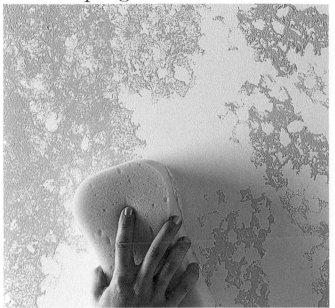

4 Working quickly, keep sponging until the surface is filled with sponged paint, but the base coat is still visible. (This layer will look fairly stark, but the next layer will soften it.) Let the paint dry. Wash out the paint tray and the sponge.

5 Dampen the sponge again. Pour the lighter color into the paint tray, and press the sponge into it. Remove the excess paint on a paper towel.

6 Sponge the lighter color evenly over the wall. Cover the area, but don't completely cover the base coat or the first color. Use a small chunk of the sponge to apply the lighter color in the corners and at the edges of the wall. Stand back from the wall and evaluate the effect. Sponge more paint where necessary to even out the variations. For best results, try to keep a consistent amount of paint on the sponge (inset).

How to Sponge Paint Stripes, Borders, or Panels

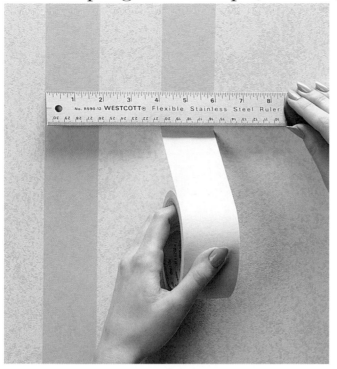

1 Apply sponge paint as described on pages 192 through 194, and let the paint dry. Tape off stripes (see page 189).

2 Apply an additional color to the unmasked areas. Blot or feather the paint, as desired. When the paint is dry, carefully remove the masking tape.

Sponging Variations

To achieve a harmonious look, use related colors for sponge painting, such as two warm colors or two cool colors. For a bolder and more unexpected look, sponge paint with a combination of warm and cool colors.

Warm and cool colors, like yellow and blue, combine boldly, but sponge painting softens the effect.

Cool colors, like green and blue, blend together for a tranquil effect.

Warm colors, like yellow and orange, blend together for an exciting effect.

Terra-cotta Finish

*I*ntroduce depth, textures, and warmth to a room by giving the walls a terra-cotta finish. Although this finish has a sophisticated appearance, it's quite easy to create, even for a beginner. Unlike many other faux finishes, a terra-cotta finish does not require a preliminary base coat. Instead, you use a wool pad to apply and blend several colors of paint. The more you blend the paints, the more muted the finish becomes. Faux finish kits and wood pads are available at paint retailers and home centers.

The finish shown here was created with three shades of latex paint: deep brown, dark clay, and apricot. The overall hue of the finish depends on the colors you choose. For a rosier finish, select colors with a red base. Or, if you prefer an orange overtone, select colors with a yellow base. If you're not sure which colors to choose, your paint retailer can help you find the right combination.

TOOLS & MATERIALS
- Divided paint tray
- Paint stirrer sticks
- Wool paint pad
- Wool finishing tool
- Brown, clay, and apricot latex paint
- Paint glaze

How to Produce a Terra-Cotta Finish with a Wool Pad

1 Pour each shade of paint into a separate section of a divided paint tray. Add a quarter cup of paint glaze to each color, blending it into the paint with a stir stick. Wet your hand with water and run it over the wool pad to remove lint and loose fibers.

2 Dip the wool pad into the brown paint, and scrape the pad along the edge of the tray to remove excess paint. Working in 4' × 4' sections, apply the paint by pressing the pad to the wall in a random pattern. Cover about 80% of the wall surface in each section, leaving some bare spots visible.

3 Scrape the pad to remove as much of the brown paint from the pad as possible. You do not need to wash the pad before applying the next paint color.

(continued next page)

4 Dip the wool pad into the clay paint, and scrape off the excess. Using the same stamping technique you used to apply the brown paint, fill in the bare spots in the section with the clay paint. When you are finished, scrape the clay paint from the pad, as before.

5 Dip the wool pad into the apricot paint, and remove the excess. Using the random stamping technique, lightly press the wool pad onto the painted section. You will begin to see the paint blend. The more you apply the apricot paint, the more the paint will blend and the lighter the final design will be.

6 Once you've finished the section, use a finishing tool to apply paint in the corners and at the edges of the section. First, remove lint and loose fibers from the tool (see Step 1). Repeat Steps 2 through 5, applying the brown, clay, and apricot paints, blending until the design is complete. When the section is complete, move on to the next.

Wool pads can be used to create a variety of finishes. Follow the same stamping technique used to create the terra-cotta finish, combining two or more colors.

Or, apply a base coat and then use a glaze-removal technique to create a dragged finish.

Tone-on-Tone: Select two paints that are three or four colors apart on a monochromatic paint selection strip, one in a dark shade and one in a light shade. Apply the dark color first. Using the random stamping technique, cover nearly all of the 4' × 4' section. Then, apply the lighter color, stamping it in until the paints are blended to create the desired effect.

Contrasting Tones: Combine a contrasting color with two shades of the same color for a bold, eye-catching pattern. Apply the same-color shades first, starting with the darker shade, then the lighter. Apply the contrasting shade last, taking care not to blend it too much. If you overblend, the colors will become muddy and you'll lose the effect of the contrasting shade.

Metallic Accent: Create a striking design by using the wool pad to apply a metallic glaze over a tone-on-tone finish. Begin by painting a tone-on-tone finish. Use another clean wool pad to lightly tap on a metallic glaze with a quick stamping motion. If you stamp too much, you'll overblend the glaze and lose the effect.

Dragged Texture: This is a glaze removal technique. Apply a base coat of paint and let it dry. Make a glaze (see page 193) and roll a coat over a 4-foot-wide strip, from the ceiling to the floor. With a clean wool pad, start at the top of the wall and drag the pad down, moving it in a straight line. Wipe the pad on a lint-free cloth, and start again at the top of the wall. Repeat until the wall is completed.

Faux Panels

Trompe l'oeil effects "fool the eye" into seeing more than is there. In this case, a chair rail and some paint imitate wood paneling, creating depth and texture on plain walls.

The trickiest part of this project is deciding on the size of the "panels." The dimensions for every project will be slightly different because the panels have to be tailored to the size of the room and length of the walls. Measure the walls in question and calculate a size that produces complete panels on as many walls as possible.

For this technique to succeed, the walls need to be in very good condition before you begin. The wood-panel effect is created by dragging and lining, both of which need to be done on smooth, flat surfaces to ensure straight lines. Prepare the walls carefully (see pages 60 through 89).

TOOLS & MATERIALS

- Large paintbrush
- 2" paintbrush
- Dragging brush
- Small fitch brush
- Ruler
- Pencil
- Carpenter's level or laser level
- Paint pail or bucket
- Pale beige matte latex paint
- Nut brown matte latex paint

How to Paint Faux Panels

1 Apply two coats of pale beige paint to the entire project area, including the chair rail. (If the room does not have a chair rail, install one 30 to 36" above the floor.)

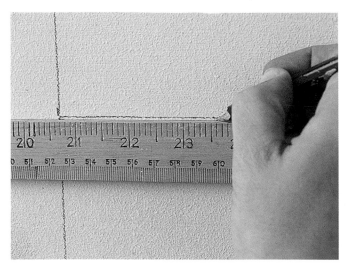

2 Measure and draw panels in proportion to the length of the wall and height of the chair rail. Use a carpenter's level or a laser level to make sure the lines are perfectly straight.

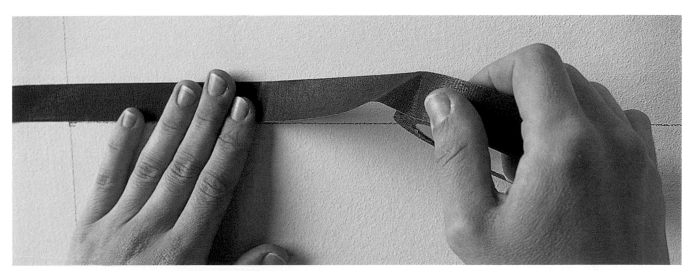

3 Mask off the horizontal "boards" above and below the central square of each panel.

4 Mix equal parts of nut brown paint and water in a pail or bucket. Dip a clean 2" paintbrush into the diluted paint and pat it on clean paper towels to remove the excess. Brush the paint vertically onto one "board" at a time.

(continued next page)

How to Paint Faux Panels *(continued)*

5 While the paint is still wet, hold a dragging brush at the top of the "board." Place your fingers near the tip of the bristles to control them, and pull the brush down through the wet paint. Keep the lines as straight as possible. Continue until you've painted and dragged all the vertical "boards" on the wall.

6 Paint and drag the central square of each panel on the wall. Remove the masking tape and allow the paint to dry.

7 Mask off the vertical panels in preparation for painting the horizontal "boards." Using the same nut-brown wash and the same dragging technique, paint and drag the horizontal parts of the panels. Drag the brush through the wet paint in the same direction on each "board" on the wall. Remove the masking tape and let the paint dry.

Paint the wash over the chair rail, using long, sweeping strokes. The goal is to create the same type of "grain" on the chair rail as on the "panels."

8 Use a small brush and the nut brown wash to create shadows at the edges of the panels. Paint a narrow band around the edges of the central square to create the illusion that the areas around the square are raised.

TIP: If a drag isn't straight enough, run over the paint again while it is still wet. It can be helpful to hang a plumb bob or shoot a laser line to act as a guide while you drag.

Blended Color Bands

*T*his blending technique creates the illusion that the colors are fading into one another, an unusual and striking effect that's easy to produce and delightful in many settings.

The success of this technique depends heavily upon good color selection. Choose two paint colors that sit next to each other on the color wheel (see page 9). You'll create the third color by mixing together equal amounts of each. The resulting midtone will smooth the transition between the top and bottom bands and enhance the illusion.

The paint has to be wet in order to blend the bands properly, so it's best to work on short sections at a time. If the paint gets too dry to blend the way you want, add fresh paint to each band, and blend it again.

TOOLS & MATERIALS

- Carpenter's level or laser level
- Tape measure
- Straightedge
- Pencil
- Five 3" paintbrushes
- Power drill and paint-mixing bit
- Three paint pails
- Two colors of matte latex paint
- Wallpaper paste

How to Create Blended Color Bands

1 Measure the wall and divide it into three equal sections. Using a laser or carpenter's level, draw horizontal lines to act as guidelines for the bands of paint.

2 Pour equal amounts of each color into a pail and use a drill and paint-mixing bit to blend it thoroughly. In a second pail, mix equal amounts of the darkest paint and wallpaper paste. In a third, mix equal amounts of the lightest paint and wallpaper paste. Label the pails.

3 Paint a 2'- to 3' section of the darkest color at the bottom of the wall, spreading the paint roughly up to the first guideline.

(continued next page)

How to Create Blended Color Bands (continued)

4 Apply a coat of the blended midtone (created in Step 2) to a 2'- to 3' section of the middle band. Leave an inch or so between this band and the first one.

5 Apply a thick coat of the dark wash to the gap between the first and second bands. Dampen a clean paintbrush and run it along the line between the bands, blending the wash up and down into each band until the lines have disappeared into a subtle transition between colors.

6 Apply the lightest color to the top band, leaving a gap between it and the middle band. Apply a thick coat of the light wash between the bands, and then use a clean, damp paintbrush to blend the colors up and down as before.

7 Continue painting one section of the wall at a time, running over at the corners. Use the finished corner as a placement guide for the newly painted one, blending the edges to make sure the color shifts are consistent. Slight variations are inevitable, but try to keep the blends as consistent as possible.

Color Wash Finishes

Color washing is an easy finish that gives walls a translucent, water-colored look. It adds visual texture to flat surfaces and can emphasize textured surfaces. There are two basic methods of color washing, each with its own glaze mixture and appearance.

The sponge method of color washing calls for a highly diluted glaze that is applied over a base coat of low-luster latex enamel, using a natural sea sponge. The result is a subtle texture with a soft blending of colors. The other method is color washing with a paintbrush, using a heavier glaze that holds more color than the sponge glaze. This finish retains the fine lines of the brush strokes to create a more dramatic play of tones. As the glaze begins to dry, it can be softened further by brushing the surface with a dry, natural-bristle paintbrush.

The color wash glaze can be either lighter or darker than the base coat. For best results, use two colors that are closely related, or consider using a neutral color, like beige or white, for either the base coat or the glaze. Because the glaze is messy to work with, cover the floor and furniture with drop cloths, and apply painter's tape along the ceiling and moldings.

TOOLS & MATERIALS

- Paint roller
- Flat latex paint, for glaze
- Latex paint conditioner, for sponge glaze
- Pail
- Natural sea sponge or two 3" to 4" natural-bristle paintbrushes
- Rubber gloves
- Painter's masking tape
- Waterproof drop cloths
- Low-luster latex enamel paint, for base coat

How to Color Wash with a Sponge

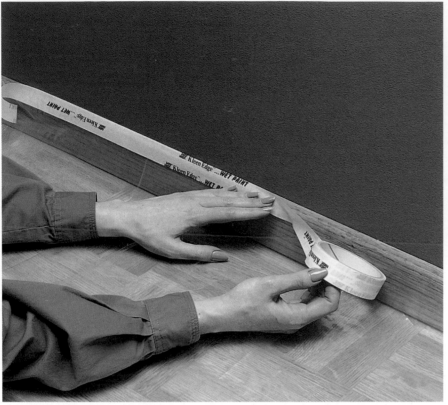

1 Mask off the surrounding area, using painter's masking tape, and cover the floor with waterproof drop cloths. Apply a base coat of low-luster latex enamel paint, using a paint roller. Allow the paint to dry.

SPONGE COLOR WASH GLAZE

Mix together the following ingredients:
- 1 part latex or acrylic paint
- 8 parts water

BRUSH COLOR WASH GLAZE

Mix together the following ingredients:
- 1 part flat latex paint
- 1 part latex paint conditioner
- 2 parts water

2 Immerse the sponge into the color-washing solution. Squeeze out excess liquid, but leave the sponge very wet.

3 Beginning in a low corner, wipe the color wash solution onto the wall in short, curving strokes. Overlap and change the direction of the strokes, quickly covering a 3' × 3' section of wall.

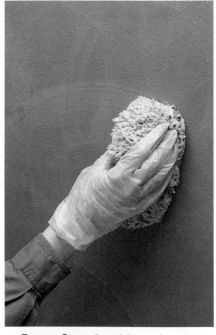

4 Repeat Steps 2 and 3, moving upward and outward until the entire wall has been color washed. Allow the paint to dry. Apply a second coat if additional color is desired.

How to Color Wash with a Brush

1 Apply a base coat of low-luster latex enamel, using a paint roller. Allow the paint to dry. Mix the color-washing glaze in a pail. Dip a paintbrush into the glaze, and remove excess glaze by scraping the brush against the rim of the pail. Apply the glaze to the wall in a cross-hatching manner, beginning in one corner. The more you brush, the softer the appearance will be.

2 Brush over the surface if desired, using a dry natural-bristle paintbrush, to soften the look. Wipe excess glaze from the brush as necessary.

Color Wash Variations

Select colors for the base coat and the glaze that are closely related, or use at least one neutral color. A darker glaze over a lighter base coat gives a mottled effect. A lighter glaze over a darker base coat gives a chalky or watercolored effect.

Here, a medium turquoise top coat was applied over a lighter base coat of white.

This finish was created with a coral base coat covered with a white top coat.

Stamped Mosaic

Mosaic tile is a classic choice for walls, but tile can be expensive and time-consuming to install. A painted mosaic is inexpensive and easy to do, and can be changed just as easily as it can be created.

The effect of a tile mosaic is too dramatic to use it in large spaces. Typically, it's best to choose a small area or the space below a chair rail for this finish. With its irregular coloration and varied pattern, a painted mosaic can cover many flaws, so the preparation steps for this project don't have to be quite as elaborate as for many other paint projects.

Apply two coats of paint to the entire wall, including the chair rail. Let the second coat dry completely, and then mask off the edges of the chair rail and baseboard.

TOOLS & MATERIALS

- Craft knife
- Large paintbrush
- Roller and roller tray
- Three I" brushes
- Small artist's brush
- Ruler
- Repositionable spray glue
- High-density foam rubber
- Low-tack masking tape
- Three colors of latex paint

How to Create a Stamped Mosaic

1 Place some of each paint color into the well of a clean roller tray. Using three clean paintbrushes, dab a generous amount of each color of paint onto the flat surface of the roller tray. It's fine for the colors to blend a little in a few places, but don't deliberately mix them.

2 To make a paper template for the stamp, draw a series of tiles divided by quarter-inch grout lines. Round the corners of the squares to resemble tile. Spray the back of the paper with repositionable spray glue and press the pattern onto the high-density foam. Cut around each tile, using a craft knife, and remove the excess pieces. (Try to consistently cut about halfway into the foam.) When the stamp is complete, press it into the paint until it's well coated but not dripping with paint.

3 Start in the top, left-hand corner of the area to be decorated. Press the stamp squarely against the wall, being careful not to let it slip. After a moment, peel the stamp away from the wall, pulling it back from one side. Recoat the stamp and position it next to the previous print. Leave a quarter-inch gap to create a grout line. Continue stamping until the project is complete. When stamping below a previous row, align the pattern lines before pressing the stamp to the wall. When adding more paint to the tray, keep the colors separate enough to create the mottled effect you're working toward. If the tiles bleed together, reestablish the base color with a small artist's brush (inset).

Stenciled Designs

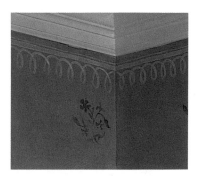

Stenciled motifs can be used to highlight an area or feature of a room or to mimic architectural details such as chair rails or crown molding.

Before beginning a project, carefully plan the placement of the design. Measure the walls and create an arrangement that doesn't produce any partial repeats. When you've come up with a plan, stencil the design on paper and tape it to the wall to make sure it works as planned. Start in the most prominent area, and work outward. If it's necessary to avoid interruptions, such as windows, doors, or heating vents, you can slightly alter the spacing between repeats to accommodate them.

Most precut stencils have a separate plate for each color and are numbered according to the sequence of use. A single plate sometimes is used for several colors if the spaces between the design areas are large enough to be covered with masking tape. When using stencils of this type, apply the largest part of the design first. When stenciling borders, it's generally best to apply all the repeats of the first color before applying the second color.

You can make custom stencils by tracing designs onto transparent Mylar sheets and cutting them out. To coordinate stencils with home furnishing such as wallpaper, fabric, or artwork, use a photocopy machine to enlarge or reduce the patterns to the desired size, and then adapt a design from them.

For painting hard surfaces, such as walls and woodwork, use craft acrylic paint or oil-based stencil paint in liquid or solid form. After stenciling over finished wood, apply a coat of clear finish or sealer to the entire surface.

How to Make a Custom Stencil

1 Draw or trace the design onto a sheet of paper. Repeat the design, if necessary, so it is 13" to 18" long, making sure the spacing between repeats is consistent. Color the design, using colored pencils. Mark placement lines to help you position the stencil on the wall.

2 Position a Mylar sheet over the design so the edges of the sheet extend beyond the top and bottom of the design by at least 1". Secure the sheet with masking tape. Trace the areas that will be stenciled in the first color, using a marking pen. Transfer the placement lines.

3 Trace the design areas for each additional color onto a separate Mylar sheet. To help you align the stencil, outline the areas for previous colors with dotted lines. Layer all of the Mylar sheets, and check for accuracy. Using a mat knife and straightedge, trim the outer edges of the stencil plates, leaving a 1" to 3" border around the design.

TOOLS & MATERIALS

- Paper
- Colored pencils
- Transparent Mylar sheets
- Masking tape
- Fine-point permanent-ink marking pen
- Cutting surface, such as a self-healing cutting board or cardboard
- Mat knife
- Metal ruler

4 Separate the Mylar sheets. Cut out the traced areas on each sheet, using a mat knife. Cut the smallest shapes first, then cut the larger ones. Pull the knife toward you as you cut, turning the Mylar sheet, rather than the knife, to change the cutting direction.

How to Stencil on Hard Surfaces

TOOLS & MATERIALS

- Carpenter's level and pencil
- Stencil brushes
- Artist's brush
- Precut or custom stencil
- Masking tape
- Spray adhesive, optional
- Craft acrylic paints, or liquid or solid oil-based stencil paints
- Clear wood finish and paintbrush if stenciling on wood
- Disposable plates
- Paper towels

1 Mark the placement for the stencil on the surface with masking tape. Or, draw a light reference line, using a carpenter's level and a pencil. Position the stencil plate for the first color, aligning the placement line with the tape or pencil line. Secure the stencil in place, using masking tape or spray adhesive.

Stenciling Variation

2 Place 1 to 2 tsp. of acrylic or oil-based paint on a disposable plate. Dip the tip of a stencil brush into the paint. Blot the brush onto a folded paper towel, using a circular motion, until the bristles are almost dry.

To stencil with solid paint, or crayon paint, remove the protective coating from the crayon tip, using a paper towel. Rub a 1½" circle of paint onto a blank area of the stencil. Load a stencil brush by lightly rubbing the brush over the paint in a circular motion, first in one direction, then in the other direction.

(continued next page)

3 Hold the brush perpendicular to the surface. Apply the paint within the cut areas of the stencil, using a circular motion. Stencil all of the cut areas of the first stencil plate, and allow the paint to dry. Remove the stencil.

4 Secure the second plate to the surface, matching the design. Apply the second paint color in all of the cut areas. Repeat the process for any remaining stencils and colors until the design is completed.

5 After all of the paints are completely dry, touch up any glitches or smudges on the surface, using background paint and an artist's brush.

Stenciling Variation

While the circular method of stenciling results in a blended finish, the stippling method produces a deeper, textured appearance. To stipple, wrap masking tape around the bristles of a stenciling brush, ¼" from the ends. Hold the brush perpendicular to the surface, and apply the paint using a dabbing motion. This method is also used to stencil fabric.

Techniques for Shaded Designs

Apply paint within the cut areas of the stencil, leaving the centers lighter than the edges. For an aged, fade-away effect, use a heavier touch at the base of the motif and a lighter touch at the top.

Apply a complementary or darker color of paint, shading the outer edges of the cut areas.

Apply paint to the outer edges of the cut areas and allow it to dry. Hold a piece of Mylar in place to cover a portion of the area, and apply paint next to the edge of the Mylar. For example, cover one-half of a leaf to stencil the veins.

Tip

Clean stencil brushes used to apply acrylic paints by applying a small amount of dishwashing detergent to the brush. Rub the bristles in the palm of your hand in a circular motion until all of the paint is removed. Rinse with water and allow the bristles to dry. To remove oil-based paint, first clean the brush with mineral spirits and dry it on paper towels. Then, wash the brush with detergent and rinse with water.

Scumbled Wall Designs

Scumbling is a simple painting technique you can use to create textural geometric patterns that mimic the look of expensive wallcovering. With this technique, a large stencil brush is used to dry-brush paint onto the wall in swirling motions over a base coat. Because very little paint is required for dry-brushing, small jars of acrylic craft paints can be used. Choose two or three related decorator colors. Or, for a look that is classic and rich, use gold and silver metallic paints.

You can customize the geometric design, covering an entire wall, as shown in the diamond design on the opposite page. Or plan a chair rail in a block pattern, a ceiling border made of triangular shapes, or a striped wainscoting. Use painter's masking tape to mask off the designs.

Measure each wall, and sketch the geometric design on graph paper to help you determine the scale and placement of the design. Before painting the walls, experiment with the painting technique, making test samples on sheets of cardboard.

To prepare the surface, clean the walls, removing any dirt or grease, and rinse them with clear water. If the walls are unfinished, apply a primer and allow it to dry thoroughly before applying the masking tape.

TOOLS & MATERIALS

- Ruler
- Pencil
- Paint roller
- Carpenter's level
- Straightedge
- Putty knife
- Stencil brush, 1" in diameter
- Graph paper
- Painter's masking tape
- Latex paint, for base coat
- Latex or craft acrylic paints, for scumbling
- Disposable plates
- Paper towels

How to Paint a Taped-off Scumbled Design

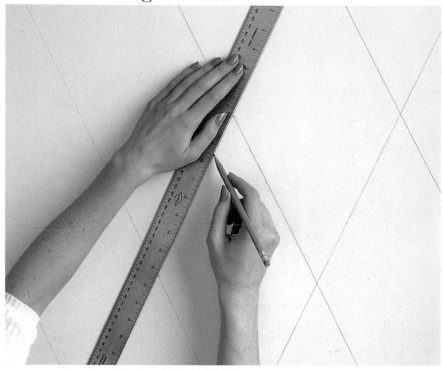

1 Measure the wall, and plan the design to scale on graph paper. Apply a base coat of paint, using a paint roller.

2 Allow the paint to dry. Draw the design on the wall with pencil, using a straight-edge as a guide.

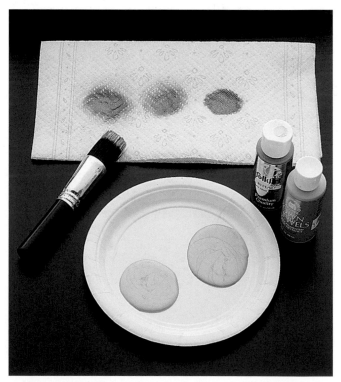

3 Mark the sections that will be masked off. Apply painter's masking tape to the marked sections, using a putty knife to trim the tape diagonally at the corners. Press along all edges of the tape, using a plastic credit card or your fingernail to create a tight seal.

4 Pour a small amount of each paint color onto a disposable plate. Dip the tip of the stencil brush into the first color. Using a circular motion, blot the brush onto a paper towel until the bristles are almost dry.

5 Brush the paint onto the wall with vigorous, wide, circular motions. Work in a small area at a time, and change the direction of the circular motions frequently. Overlap the paint onto the masking tape. Build up the color to the desired intensity, but allow the base coat to show through. Use all of the paint on bristles before applying more.

6 Dip the brush into the second color, and blot the brush. Apply the paint randomly over the same area, building up the color to varying intensities throughout the area. Repeat with a third color, if desired.

7 Repeat the technique to complete the entire wall, working in one small area at a time and blending areas together. Remove the masking tape when the paint is dry.

Strié & Combed Finishes

Strié and combed finishes are created by similar techniques in which a tool is dragged over wet glaze to reveal a base coat of a different color. The result is a textured, linear pattern, which can run in vertical lines, curves, swirls, zig-zags, or a weave pattern resembling fabric. Both finishes start with a base coat of low-luster latex enamel, followed by a latex or acrylic glaze mixture. The differences between these finishes are the result of the tools used to create the pattern.

The strié effect is created using a dry, natural-bristle brush, resulting in fine, irregular streaks and an interesting blend of color variations. A combed finish can be made with a variety of specialty tools, offering a range of patterns and designs. An additional option for the combed finish is to use a thickened glaze, which gives an opaque look and more distinct lines and texture.

Since the glaze must be wet for brushing or combing, timing is important with both techniques. For large surfaces, it is helpful to work with an assistant. After one person has applied the glaze, the other person brushes or combs through the glaze before it dries. If you are working alone, limit yourself to smaller sections. For best results, practice the technique and experiment with different glaze thicknesses by testing the finish on mat board before painting the wall.

TOOLS & MATERIALS

- Paint roller or natural-bristle paintbrush
- Wide natural-bristle brush
- Soft natural-bristle paintbrush
- Combing tool
- Low-luster latex enamel, for base coat
- Latex paint in desired sheen and color, for glaze
- Latex paint conditioner, such as Floetrol
- Rags

BASIC GLAZE
Mix together the following ingredients:
   1 part latex or craft acrylic paint
   1 part latex paint conditioner
   1 part water

THICKENED GLAZE
Mix together the following ingredients:
   2 parts latex or craft acrylic paint
   1 part acrylic paint thickener (may be used with latex paints)

How to Apply a Strié Paint Finish

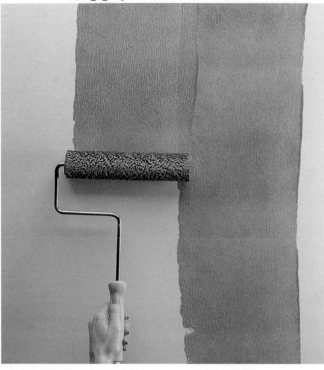

1 Apply the base coat of low-luster latex enamel, and allow the paint to dry. Mix the glaze (page 223). Apply the glaze over the base coat in a vertical section about 18" wide, using a paint roller or natural-bristle paintbrush.

2 Drag a dry, wide natural-bristle brush through the wet glaze, immediately after the glaze is applied; work from top to the bottom in continuous brush strokes. To keep the brush rigid, hold the bristles against the surface with the handle tilted slightly toward you. Repeat until the desired effect is achieved.

3 Wipe the paintbrush occasionally on a clean, dry rag to re-move excess glaze and ensure a uniform strié look. Or, rinse the brush in clear water, and wipe it dry.

4 For softer lines, brush the surface lightly after the glaze has dried for about 5 minutes. Use a soft natural-bristle brush, keeping the brush stokes in the same direction as the streaks.

Techniques for Applying a Combed Finish

Tools for combing include the Wagner Stipple and Drag pad (with edging tool), metal and rubber combs, and a notched rubber squeegee. You can make your own combing tools by notching an artist's eraser or cutting V grooves into a piece of mat board.

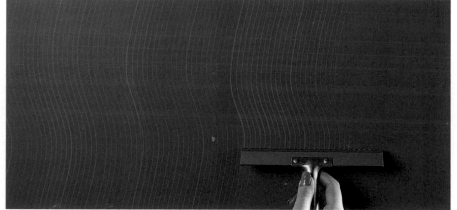

Create a unique check pattern, using a rubber comb. After each pass, wipe off the tool with a dry rag to prevent the glaze from building up and smearing the comb lines.

A Wagner Stipple and Drag pad can make a variety of combing designs. For a denim look, drag the pad through the glaze vertically, then horizontally

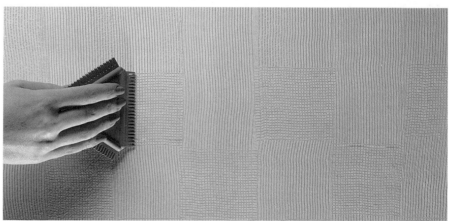

Use a rubber squeegee for swirls, scallops, and wavy lines. Wipe off excess glaze frequently to ensure clean lines.

Faux Moiré Finish

*T*he watermarked look of silk moiré fabric can be created using a rocker tool designed for wood graining (page 182). A paint glaze is applied over a base coat of paint, and the graining tool is pulled and rocked through the glaze to create impressions. Then, a dry paintbrush is pulled across the markings to mimic the crosswise grain of moiré. This dramatic tone-on-tone finish is recommended for small areas, such as the space below a chair rail or within frame moldings.

The bright sheen that is characteristic of moiré fabric is simulated by using a darker shade of low-luster latex enamel for the base coat and a lighter shade for the top coat glaze. You can use the same paint for both coats by lightening the top coat with white paint.

The glaze used for faux moiré contains more paint than most glazes, making it thicker and more opaque. Apply the glaze to a small area at a time so that you will have enough time to finish the graining before the glaze dries. If you are finishing the wall area below a chair rail or border, work from the chair rail down to the baseboard in 12"-wide sections.

TOOLS & MATERIALS

- Wood-graining rocker tool
- Paint roller or paintbrush, for applying base coat and glaze
- Natural-bristle paintbrush, 2" to 3" wide, for dry brushing
- Low-luster latex enamel paint in darker shade, for base coat
- Low-luster enamel paint in lighter shade, or white paint to lighten base color, for glaze
- Latex paint conditioner
- Rags

How to Apply a Faux Moiré Finish

FAUX MOIRÉ GLAZE

Mix together the following ingredients:
2 parts semigloss latex enamel paint
1 part latex paint conditioner
1 part water

1 Apply the base coat of low-luster latex enamel, using a paint roller or paintbrush. Allow the paint to dry.

2 Mix the glaze for the top coat. Apply an even coat of glaze over the base, rolling or brushing vertically. Work in small areas to ensure the paint remains wet as you work it.

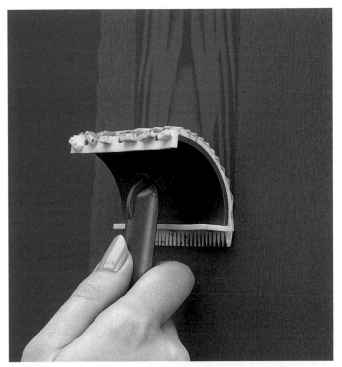

3 Slide the graining tool vertically through the wet glaze, occasionally rocking it slowly back and forth, to create the watermarked effect. Start at one corner, working in one continuous motion as you slide and rock the tool from one end to another. The simultaneous rocking and sliding motions create elongated oval markings.

4 Repeat Step 3 for subsequent rows. Stagger the oval markings so that they appear randomly placed, and work quickly before glaze dries. Wipe the excess glaze from the tool as necessary, using a dry rag.

5 When the glaze has partially dried, pull a dry natural-bristle paintbrush horizontally across the surface; this mimics the crosswise grain of the moiré fabric. Wipe excess glaze from the brush as necessary. Allow the paint to dry.

Rag-rolled Designs

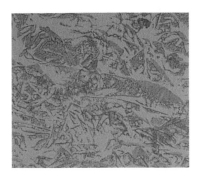

*R*ag rolling is a painting technique that gives a rich, textural look with an all-over mottled effect. It works well for walls and other flat surfaces, such as dresser tops and drawers, shelves, bookends, and doors. The rag-rolling glaze on page 232 can be used in either of the two techniques for rag rolling: *ragging-on* and *ragging-off.*

In ragging-on, a rag is saturated in the prepared paint glaze, wrung out, rolled up, then rolled across a surface that has been base-coated with low-luster latex enamel paint. For a bold pattern, rag-on a single application of glaze over the base coat. Or, for a more subtle, blended look, rag-on two or more applications of glaze.

In ragging-off, a coat of paint glaze is applied over the base coat with a paintbrush or paint roller. A rolled-up rag is then rolled over the surface to remove some of the wet glaze, revealing the base coat. This process may be repeated for more blending, but the work must be done quickly, before the glaze dries.

If you are using the ragging-off method on large surfaces, such as walls, it is helpful to have an assistant. After one person applies the glaze, the second person can rag-off the area before the glaze dries. While it is not necessary to complete the entire room in one session, it is important that you complete an entire wall.

With either method, test the technique and the colors that you intend to use on a large piece of cardboard, such as mat board, before you start the project. Generally, a lighter color is used for the base coat, with a darker color for the glaze.

Feel free to experiment with the technique as you test it, perhaps rag rolling two different glaze colors over the base coat. Or, try taping off an area, such as a border strip, and rag rolling a second or third color within the taped area.

Because the glaze can be messy to work with, apply a wide painter's tape around the area to be painted and use drop cloths to protect the surrounding surfaces. Wear old clothes and rubber gloves, and keep an old towel nearby to wipe your hands after you wring out the rags.

How to Apply a Rag-rolled Finish Using the Ragging-on Method

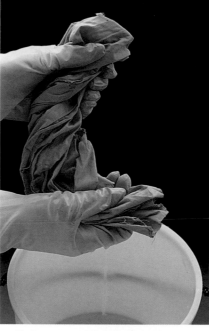

TOOLS & MATERIALS

- Paintbrush or paint roller
- Paint pail
- Paint tray
- Painter's masking tape
- Low-luster latex enamel paint, for base coat
- Latex or craft acrylic paint, for glaze
- Latex paint conditioner
- Rubber gloves
- Lint-free rags, about 24" × 24"
- Towel

RAG-ROLLING GLAZE

Mix together the following ingredients:
1 part latex or craft acrylic paint
1 part latex paint conditioner
1 part water

1 Apply a base coat of low-luster latex enamel, using a paintbrush or paint roller. Allow the paint to dry. Mix the glaze in a pail. Dip a lint-free rag into the glaze, saturating the entire rag, then wring it out well. Wipe excess glaze from your hands with an old towel.

2 Roll up the rag irregularly, then fold it to a length equal to the width of both hands.

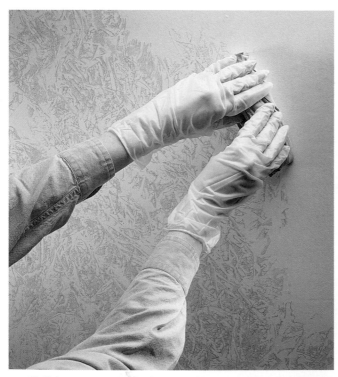

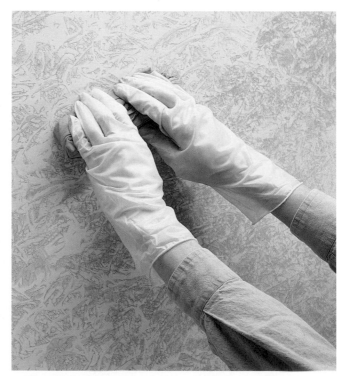

3 Roll the rag over the surface, working upward at varying angles. Rewet the rag whenever necessary, and wring it out.

4 Repeat the application, if more coverage is desired.

How to Apply a Rag-rolled Finish Using the Ragging-off Method

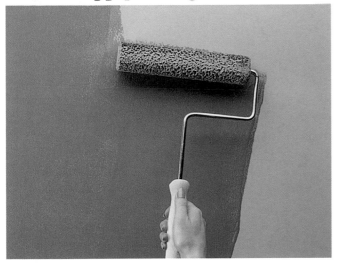

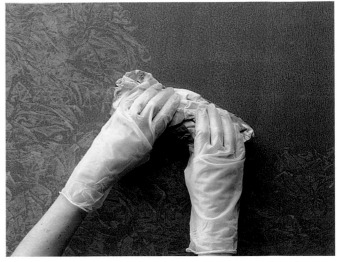

1 Apply base coat of low-luster latex enamel, using a paint-brush or paint roller. Allow the paint to dry. Mix the glaze (page opposite), and pour it into a paint tray. Apply the glaze over the base coat, using paint roller or paint pad.

2 Roll up a lint-free rag irregularly, then fold it to a length equal to the width of both hands. Roll the rag through the wet glaze, working upward at varying angles.

Rag-roll Variations

As shown in the examples below, the color of the base coat is not affected when the ragging-on method is used. With the ragging-off method, the color of the base coat is changed, because the glaze is applied over the entire surface.

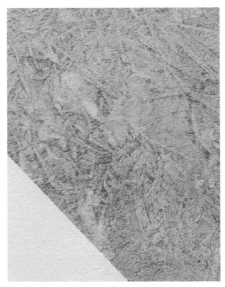

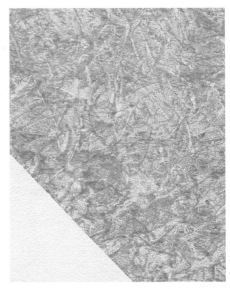

Here, the ragging-on method was used to apply an aqua glaze over a white base coat. The white base coat remained unchanged.

The ragging-off method was used here to remove some of the aqua glaze from a white base coat. Because the base was covered with the glaze, the lighter areas appear as light aqua, rather than white.

Both ragging-on and ragging-off methods were used here. First, a taupe glaze was ragged-on over a white base coat, then a rust glaze was ragged-off, changing the white base coat to a lighter shade of rust.

Faux Serpentine Finish

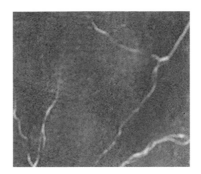

Serpentine is the general name given to a variety of green marbles that contain deposits of the mineral serpentine. The different types vary in visual texture and color tone, often with traces of black and white. Some serpentines may be characterized by a network of fine veining, while others contain little or no veining. As with other marbles, the serpentines have been used for various architectural applications, including floors, walls, and pillars.

Because genuine marble is often cut into workable pieces for installation, a faux serpentine finish applied to a large surface is more realistic if it is applied in sections with narrow grout lines. By masking off alternate sections, the finish can be applied to half the project, following Steps 1 to 8. When the first sections have been allowed to dry completely, they can be masked off, and the finish can be applied to the remaining sections. A high-gloss finish is then applied to the entire surface, giving the faux finish the lustrous appearance of genuine marble.

TOOLS & MATERIALS

- Low-napped paint roller, for base coat on a large surface
- Sponge applicator or paintbrush
- Stippler
- Spray bottle
- Turkey feather, for veining
- Medium green low-luster latex enamel paint, for base coat
- Craft acrylic paints in green (darker than base coat), black, and white
- Water-based clear urethane
- Newspaper
- Cheesecloth
- High-gloss clear finish or high-gloss aerosol clear acrylic sealer

How to Apply a Faux Serpentine Finish

FAUX SERPENTINE
GLOSS GLAZE

Mix together the following ingredients
for each gloss glaze:
   1 part clear urethane
   1 part paint, in desired shade
   1 part water

1 Apply a base coat of medium green low-luster latex enamel to the surface, using an applicator suitable to the surface size. Apply black, green, and white gloss glazes separately in random, broad, diagonal strokes, using a sponge applicator or paintbrush. Cover most of the surface, allowing small patches of the base coat to show through.

2 Stipple the glazes in adjoining areas to blend them slightly, bouncing a stippler rapidly over the surface.

3 Fold a sheet of newspaper to several layers and lay it flat over an area of the surface, in the same diagonal direction as the original paint strokes. Press the newspaper into the glaze, then lift it off, removing some of glaze.

4 Repeat Step 3 over the entire surface, using the same newspaper. Occasionally turn the paper in opposite directions. Add glazes as desired to develop the color, and soften areas of high contrast by dabbing with wadded cheesecloth. Mist the surface with water if necessary, to keep the glazes workable.

5 Brush black glaze onto a piece of newspaper and touch it to the surface diagonally in scattered areas, adding drama and depth. Soften with cheesecloth, if necessary. Repeat the process using a white glaze in small, light areas.

6 Dilute a mixture of white and green glazes with water to the consistency of light cream. Run the edge and tip of the feather through the diluted glaze. Place the tip of the feather onto the surface in the desired placement for a vein. Lightly drag the feather diagonally over the surface, fidgeting and turning it slightly, and varying the pressure, to create an irregular, jagged vein. Begin and end veins off the edge of the surface.

7 Repeat step 6 as desired to build a veining pattern. Connect adjacent vein lines occasionally to create narrow, oblong, irregular shapes. Dab veins lightly with wadded cheesecloth to soften, if necessary. Allow the surface to dry.

8 Dilute the glazes to the consistency of ink, and apply each randomly to the surface. Dab with wadded cheesecloth to soften the colors. Allow the glazes to dry. Apply several thin coats of high-gloss clear finish or high-gloss aerosol clear acrylic sealer, allowing the surface to dry between coats.

Words on Walls

The pages of high-end decorating magazines are filled with pictures of walls that talk. The walls don't literally speak, of course. Instead, they display favorite folk sayings, bits of poetry, or quotes from famous and infamous people throughout history.

If you have a favorite saying, you're ready to get to work. If not, spend some quality time with books of quotations, such as *The Oxford Book of Quotations, Bartlett's Famous Quotes* and *The Quotable Woman.* These books are filled with interesting, inspirational quotes from a wide variety of sources. So, too, are Internet sites that feature quotations. Type "famous quotations" into a search engine and browse until you find something that inspires or amuses you. You're likely to live with these words for a while, so be sure to choose something that reflects your personality and interests or your sense of humor.

One key to a project like this is making the words proportional to the space where they're displayed, and that can take some trial and error. (This is where patience comes in handy.) If you're working with a soffit or other small linear space, try making the letters about two-thirds the height of the soffit. You may prefer to have the words larger or smaller, but two-thirds is a good starting point.

The font you choose should fit the room as well as the saying. A casual font with a little attitude works well for a short, funny saying. Flowing script sets the tone for poetry or sentimental thoughts. Extremely complex fonts are difficult to work with and difficult to read, so it's often best to avoid them.

TOOLS & MATERIALS

- Laser or carpenter's level
- Stylus or dull pencil
- Graphite paper
- Artist's paintbrushes
- Craft paint
- Craft paint in a slightly darker color (optional)

High-quality artist's brushes create clean lines and can be shaped to create curved lines and shadows.

How to Paint Words on Walls

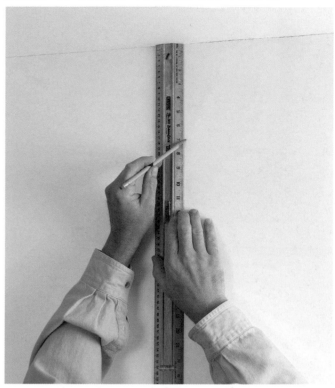

1 Measure the available space and evaluate the quotations you're considering. Imagine where you would break the lines and how you want the words stacked or displayed.

2 If necessary, fill any holes or dents in the wall and repair any cracks. Prime and paint the wall with two coats of eggshell or flat latex paint.

3 On a computer, select a font and size, and create a design for the words. Refer to the wall measurements taken in Step 1, and arrange the words of the quotation to fit.

(continued next page)

Advanced Paint Designs & Finishes   239

4 Print out the quotation and trim away the edges of the paper. Tape the printouts on the wall and evaluate the size and placement of the words. Keep trying sizes and arrangements until you're satisfied.

5 Set up a laser level to shoot a baseline for the words onto the wall. If you don't have a laser level, use a carpenter's level or a bubblestick and a pencil to create a faint line.

6 Hold a piece of graphite paper against the wall, and tape the printout over it. (Be sure you're using graphite paper, not carbon paper. It doesn't smudge.) Line up the base of the letters with the laser line or pencil guideline.

7 Trace the words, using a stylus or other blunt tool with a blunt end. The goal is to create a pattern line without tearing the printout or the graphite paper. Remove the printouts and graphite paper and check the pattern lines. Fill out any faint lines or skipped areas with a pencil.

8 Pour a small puddle of the lighter paint color onto a plastic palette. Dampen an angled paintbrush with water and pat it on a clean paper towel. Dip the corner of the long side of the brush into the craft paint and draw it across the palette to get the paint flowing smoothly.

9 Paint the large, straight, open areas of the letters. Wash out the brush in plain water about every other time you load it, and continue to load only the long side of the brush with paint. If you have to stop in the middle of the project, wash out the brush with soap and water and reshape it before it dries.

10 Use a round-tip brush to paint the curved portions of the letters. Dampen the brush and load only one side with paint. Pull the brush across the palette to distribute the paint evenly, as you did with the angled brush. Draw the brush along the pencil lines, pushing down slightly more as you sweep around curves. The brush should flow along the curves and leave graceful, accurate lines.

Variation: Wash the palette and the angled brush. Pour a small puddle of the darker paint onto the palette and load one side of the damp brush with it. Stroke the brush across the palette until the paint blends with the water on the brush and runs from dark on the long side of the brush to light on the other side. Lightly sweep the brush around the inside edges and curves of the letters, creating a slight shadow.

Decorating with Advanced Techniques

*J*ust as modern paints and glazes make it possible for do-it-yourselfers to achieve wonderful custom paint finishes, there is a wide range of new wallcovering and molding products now available that let you add exciting architectural dimensions to your decorating scheme. In this section of the book, we'll show you three techniques for giving your home a truly hand-crafted look.

Specialty wallcoverings, such as fabrics and embossed materials, can be fragile and difficult to work with, as well as expensive, but their natural or textured surfaces add more than just color to a wall. On the following pages, we'll give you some essential tips for preparing your walls and show you how to handle and install specialty materials for flawless results.

Decorative moldings add a permanent elegance to an interior space, and do-it-youselfers now have many options to choose from. For example, you can create wall frame moldings using basic wood trim available at any home center. Or, you can choose from among the many new polyurethane products now available from specialty retailers and catalog vendors. Whichever products you choose, this section will show you the tools and basic installation techniques you'll need do the job.

Specialty Wallcoverings

Specialty wallcoverings can add new interest to a room. The basic hanging methods are the same as for standard wall-coverings (pages 142–179), but specialty wallcoverings do require some special handling techniques. Reflective wallcoverings, such as foils and Mylars, can add light to even the darkest rooms, but the walls must be perfectly smooth before hanging. Fabric or grasscloth wallcoverings can soften and hide flaws in irregular walls, but they are difficult to keep clean. Embossed wallcoverings also hide flawed walls, but do not soil as easily as fabrics and grasscloths.

For very rough walls, consider hanging a liner paper before the wallcovering. Liner paper strips are hung horizontally so that the wallcovering seams cannot overlap the liner seams.

Always follow the manufacturer's directions when hanging specialty wallcoverings, and make your selection carefully: Specialty wallcoverings can be expensive.

Tips for Working with Fabric Wallcoverings

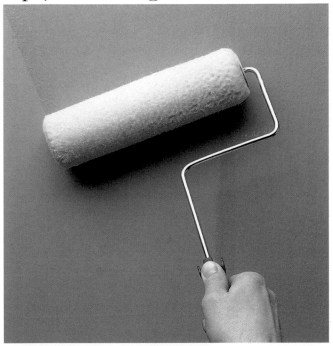

Use a clear adhesive or traditional wheat paste, as directed by the manufacturer. Clear adhesive will not bleed through and stain fabric surfaces. Some wallcoverings may direct you to apply adhesive to the walls rather than to the strips.

Use a dry paint roller with a soft nap, or a soft brush with natural bristles to smooth flocks and fabrics. A brush with stiff bristles might damage the wallcovering surface.

Tips for Working with Foil Wallcoverings

Apply liner paper to create a smooth base for wallcovering over rough or uneven surfaces, such as paneled, textured or masonry walls.

Handle foils carefully. Do not crease or wrinkle the strips, and make sure to flatten out all bubbles immediately when hanging.

Use a soft smoothing brush to avoid scratching or burnishing the reflective surface. Do not roll the seams: tap gently with a smoothing brush to bond seams.

Tips for Working with Embossed Wallcoverings

Apply a clay-based wallcovering adhesive to the back side of the wallcovering strips, using a paint roller. Take care not to press the roller too hard against the paper. Too much pressure can damage the embossed pattern.

Gently tap seams with a smoothing brush to bond them. Do not use a seam roller on embossed wallcoverings.

Keep adhesive off the face of embossed wallcoverings if possible. Remove wet adhesive immediately by blotting gently with a slightly damp sponge.

Finish embossed wallcoverings with several coats of latex paint. Use a paintbrush, working the paint evenly into the crevices. Let the paint dry between coats.

Embossed Wallcovering Finish Variations

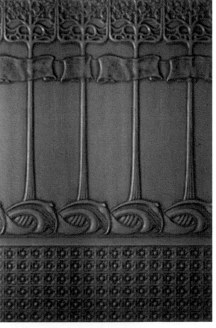

Clouding finish: Apply two coats of alkyd paint for the base tone. Combine a darker, related shade of alkyd paint with clear glaze, applying it over the first coat.

Gold highlighting: Start by priming the wallcovering with acrylic primer. Then, apply two coats of latex eggshell finish paint for the base coat. Apply a gold glaze to the raised details with a small artist's brush.

Wiped finish: Apply an undercoat of acrylic white primer, followed by two coats of white alkyd paint. Combine high gloss enamel in the desired overtone with clear glaze, and "wipe" it onto the surface with a cotton rag.

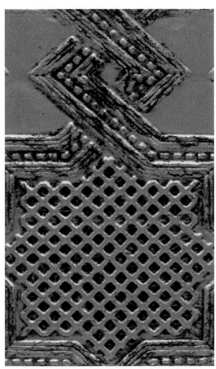

Faux tin finish: Apply two coats of satin latex in white, one coat of latex metallic paint in silver, one coat of oak-toned glaze, and a final coat of semigloss varnish.

Antiqued leather finish: Apply two coats of satin latex as a base tone, followed by a coat of dark-toned glaze applied in small sections. Partially remove the glaze with a cotton rag. Finish with a final coat of semigloss varnish.

Wall Frame Moldings

*A*dd architectural detail to a living room by installing molding in a picture-type frame on the walls. Frame molding can be used to accent special features of the room, divide large walls into smaller sections, and add interest to otherwise plain walls. The molding may be the same color as the walls, or a contrasting color. The effect can be intensified by painting the wall area within the frame molding a different color or by applying a wallcovering to the inset area.

Simple, decorative wood moldings, available at home centers and lumber yards in a wide variety of styles, work best for wall frames. To determine the size and location of the frames, cut strips of paper the width of the molding and experiment with different frame sizes by taping the strips to the wall. Where possible, try to size the frame molding so it matches the dimension of some architectural detail in the room—such as the width of windows or a fireplace.

Install the molding with small finish nails near the outside corners of the molding and at wall stud locations; use nails long enough to go through the wall surface and into the studs. If you aren't able to locate wall studs where you need them, apply small dots of wood glue or construction adhesive to the back of the molding to secure the frame pieces to the wall.

TOOLS & MATERIALS

- Wood molding
- Butcher paper, for strips
- Masking tape
- Carpenter's level and pencil
- Measuring tape
- Miter box and backsaw, or power miter saw
- Drill and 1/16" bit

- 6d finish nails
- Hammer
- Nail set
- Wood glue or construction adhesive, if necessary
- Paint and paintable latex caulk, or wood stain and putty to match stain
- Paintbrush

How to Install Wall Frame Moldings

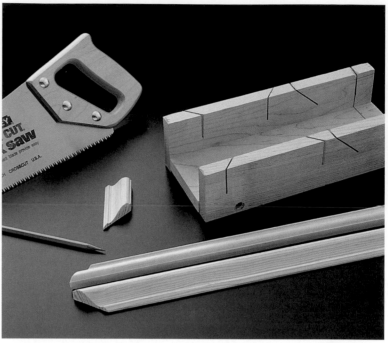

1 Cut paper strips to the width of the molding, and tape them to the wall. Mark the placement for the outer edge of the top molding piece with light pencil lines. Use a carpenter's level to make sure the marks are level.

2 Measure and mark 45° cutting lines on the upper and lower molding pieces. Cut the pieces, using a miter box and a back saw. The top and bottom pieces should be the same length. Repeat to cut the side strips. Test-fit the first molding, and if satisfied, cut pieces for all other moldings to match the dimensions of the first pieces.

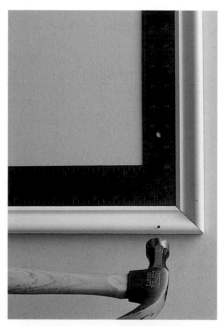

3 Paint or stain the moldings, as desired. Drill pilot holes with a 1/16" drill bit. Position the top molding piece on the wall, aligning it with the placement marks. Apply small dots of glue to the back of the molding, where necessary. Nail the moldings to the wall, leaving the nail heads slightly above the surface.

4 Attach the side molding pieces, placing a partially driven nail at the upper ends only. Fit the bottom piece, making sure the frame is square. Adjust the frame, if necessary, so that all of the joints fit tightly at the corners. Then, secure the pieces with nails and glue.

5 Drive the nails slightly below the surface, using a nail set. Fill the nail holes and corner joints with paintable latex caulk if the molding is painted, or wood putty if it is stained. Touch up the patched areas with paint or stain.

Wall Frame Molding Variations

These framed areas are wallcovered, creating depth and interest in an otherwise plain wall.

The double moldings on this wall emphasize the architectural detailing.

Contrasting molding calls special attention to the artwork in this traditional grouping.

Decorative Moldings

*A*dd a dramatic accent to a room with polyurethane moldings. Polyurethane moldings have the look of cast plaster and hand-carved wood moldings but are lighter and easier to install than moldings made with traditional materials. Polyurethane products are manufactured to replicate historical styles for a variety of architectural elements, including crown and trim moldings, ceiling medallions, pilasters, corbels, and raised panels.

Polyurethane moldings can be painted the same color as the walls or ceiling, painted with a contrasting color, decorated with a faux finish design, or treated with a wood stain. Another option is to highlight the intricate raised designs by painting the raised patterns in one or more contrasting colors.

Using a special adhesive, you can attach polyurethane moldings to most interior surfaces. To ensure good adhesion and an even finish, you'll need to prepare the surface—clean the walls, remove any old wallcovering, repair loose or damaged plaster or wallboard, and prime or sand the surface (see pages 60–89). To prevent warping, store the moldings in the room where they will be installed for 24 hours prior to installation. Avoid installing the molding when the humidity level is greater than 70%.

When installing patterned moldings, begin the installation at the most visible corner so that you can easily match the pattern. Finish the installation at an inconspicuous corner, where an unmatched pattern will be less obvious.

How to Install a Ceiling Medallion Above a Chandelier

A ceiling medallion is an elegant accent that can highlight a chandelier or other light fixture and establish a visual center point in a room. Removing a chandelier is easy and safe if you make sure to turn off the power to the fixture at the main service panel and have a helper support the weight of the chandelier while you disconnect it.

To determine how your chandelier is supported, examine the decorative coverplate at the ceiling. There should be either a retaining nut in the center, or two or more nuts or screws on the surface of the coverplate. This hardware may support the weight of the fixture, so have a helper support the fixture as you remove the nuts and the coverplate.

TOOLS & MATERIALS

- Screwdriver, adjustable wrench, or channel-type pliers
- Pencil
- Drill, circle cutter, piloting and countersink bits
- Caulk gun
- Cordless screwdriver
- Polyurethane ceiling medallion
- 150-grit sandpaper
- Polyurethane adhesive
- Wallboard screws
- Paintable latex caulk or filler

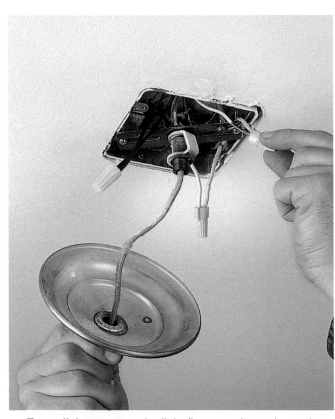

1 Turn off the power to the light fixture at the main service panel. Unscrew the coverplate retaining nut or screws and lower the coverplate to expose the wire connections. Disconnect the fixture wires from the home's circuit wires by removing the wire connectors. The fixture wire marked with lettering or a colored stripe is the neutral wire; it is connected to the white circuit wire. The unmarked fixture wire is hot and is connected to the black circuit wire.

Most chandeliers are supported by a threaded nipple that is screwed into a mounting strap attached to the electrical box. Unscrew this nipple and set the fixture out of the way. If the fixture is supported by a coverplate that is screwed or bolted directly to the mounting strap, you can remove the fixture once the wires are disconnected.

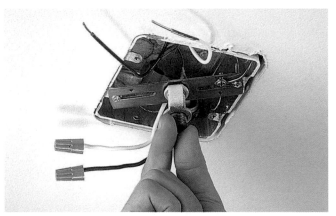

2 To compensate for the added thickness of the medallion, unscrew the threaded nipple and replace it with a longer one, or buy longer screws that will reach from the coverplate to the mounting strap.

3 Lightly sand the back of the medallion with 150-grit sandpaper. Adjust a circle cutter to cut a hole through the medallion that is smaller than the chandelier coverplate but large enough to provide access to the screw holes on the mounting strap. Cut the hole for the center of the medallion, using the circle cutter and a power drill. Position the medallion on the ceiling, centering the hole over the electrical box, and draw a light pencil line to mark its placement on the ceiling.

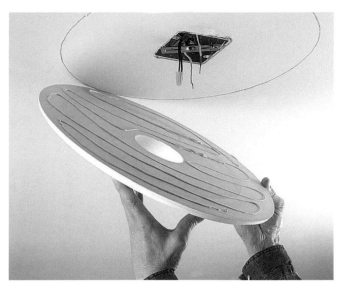

4 Apply polyurethane adhesive to the back of the medallion. Run the bead in a serpentine pattern and keep the adhesive 1" away from the outer edge of the medallion. Carefully align the medallion within the penciled outline and press it onto the ceiling. Drill several countersunk pilot holes through the medallion in inconspicuous areas. Then, drive wallboard screws through the pilot holes and into the ceiling to hold the medallion in place while the glue dries. Be careful not to tighten the screws too much.

5 Fill the screw holes with paintable latex caulk or filler, and wipe away any excess caulk with a damp cloth or a wet finger. Smooth the caulk over the holes so it is flush with the surface of the medallion. Paint or stain the medallion, if desired, and let the finish dry completely. Reattach the chandelier.

Molding Finish Variations

The great variety of polyurethane moldings allows you to combine styles and architectural elements for a distinctive decorative addition to any room.

Here, raised panels add depth to the flat wall and door surfaces. The door frame is trimmed with pilasters, a lintel, and corner blocks. On the wall, a sconce provides a pleasing fan of light.

This wall is topped with an elaborate cornice molding. Crown and cornice moldings can be combined with other types of trim, such as casing, base, and panel moldings, to enhance the design.

In this scheme, the intricate detail of the ceiling medallion is offset by the Victorian crown molding. A classical corbel serves as a decorative anchor for the archway.

How to Install Crown Molding

TOOLS & MATERIALS

- Caulk gun
- Cordless screwdriver
- Measuring tape, pencil
- Hammer
- Putty knife
- Drill, piloting, and countersink bits
- Power miter saw or hand miter box and fine-tooth saw
- Polyurethane crown molding
- Spackling compound and putty knife
- Polyurethane adhesive
- 2" wallboard screws
- Finish nails
- Paintable latex caulk or filler

1 Plan the layout of the molding pieces by measuring the walls of the room and making light pencil marks at the joint locations. For each piece that starts or ends at a corner, add 1' to 2' to compensate for the waste resulting from miter cutting the end. Avoid pieces less than 3' long, if possible, because shorter pieces are more difficult to fit.

2 Hold a section of molding against the wall and ceiling in the finished position. Make light pencil marks on the wall every 1' along the bottom edge of the molding. Remove the molding and tack a finish nail at each pencil mark: these will hold the molding in place while the adhesive dries. If the wall is plaster, drill pilot holes for the nails.

3 Start the first molding pieces at the most conspicuous corner to be sure the pattern will match. To make the miter cuts for the first corner, position the molding face up in a miter box. Set the ceiling-side edge of the molding flat against the horizontal base of the miter box, and set the wall-side edge against the vertical back fence. Make the cut at 45°.

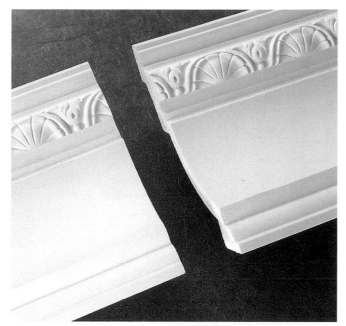

4 Check the uncut ends of each molding piece before installing it. Make sure mating pieces will butt together squarely in a tight joint. Cut all square ends at 90°, using the miter saw or hand miter box.

5 Lightly sand the back edges of the molding that will make contact with the wall and ceiling, using 150-grit sandpaper. Wipe away the sanding dust, using a rag slightly dampened with mineral spirits. Run a small bead of polyurethane adhesive along both sanded edges.

6 Set the molding in place with the mitered end tight to the corner and the bottom edge resting on the finish nails. Press along the wall and ceiling edges to create a good bond. At both ends of the molding section, drill a countersunk pilot hole through the top and bottom edges and into the ceiling and wall. Drive a wallboard screw through each pilot hole to secure the molding in place.

7 Cut, sand, and glue the next section of molding. Apply a bead of adhesive to the end of the installed molding where it will butt against the new section. Install the new section, and secure the ends with screws, making sure the joints are aligned properly. Install the remaining molding sections and allow the adhesive to dry.

8 Carefully remove the finish nails and fill the nail holes with spackling compound. Fill the screw holes in the molding and any gaps in the joints with paintable latex caulk or filler, and wipe away excess caulk with a damp cloth or a wet finger. Smooth the caulk over the holes so it is flush with the surface.

Painting Furniture

*P*ainted furniture breathes life into a room, especially pieces that have been treated to interesting finishes, such as color washes or aging techniques. A coat of paint can unlock the potential of an old or tired table or chair, completely transforming it in the space of an afternoon. It's easy, it's inexpensive, and it's fun.

Eventually, you'll be comfortable enough to work on anything that catches your eye and imagination, but it's best to start with garage sale or flea market finds rather than valuable pieces or family heirlooms.

You're bound to feel more confident working on a bargain piece than one that has been in the family for generations, and that confidence will allow you to take risks and try new techniques without fear or hesitation.

Before starting a project, take the time to gather the essential materials. Having to run to the store for supplies interferes with the momentum of a project and can sidetrack you for hours or days. It's a good idea to keep basic materials, such as a range of sandpapers, brushes, drop cloths, masking tape,

rags, and jars or cans, on hand all the time. Then, if the inspiration strikes, you can work without pause, with all the necessary materials on hand right when you need them.

Aged Finish

An aged finish confers instant character on any piece of furniture. With not much more than a wave of your magic paintbrush, you can transform an ordinary new piece of furniture into a treasure that appears to have been part of the family for generations.

The actual process of aging a finish is quite simple, but doing it well takes some planning and a little imagination. Before starting a project, look at the piece carefully and think about how it is used and which areas would show wear if it actually were old. Generally speaking, wear first appears in the areas where a piece is touched often—behind or around handles, on the edges, at the backs of seats, and in the center of the top front rung of a chair. These are the areas you should plan to distress.

Vintage pieces typically show wear in the places where they've been handled for generations. Distressing the Paint in these areas creates an authentic looking aged finish.

TOOLS & MATERIALS

- Cordless screwdriver
- 2" synthetic-bristle brush
- 1½" synthetic-bristle brush
- Putty knife
- Extra-fine sandpaper
- Tack cloth
- Soft cotton rags
- Small can of water-based wood stain
- Furniture wax
- Flat-finish latex paint in a dark color
- Flat-finish latex paint in lighter color
- Satin-finish polyurethane spray

How to Create an Aged Finish

1 Take out any drawers. Carefully remove all the hardware from the piece. Most drawer handles have a screw (or two) on the inside face of the drawer. Remove the screws and pull off the handles. When removing hinges, support the door as you remove the screws.

2 Lightly sand the surface with fine-grit sandpaper. Sand—in the direction of the grain—until the surface is smooth and even. Remove the sanding dust with tack cloth.

3 Stain the entire piece with dark water-based stain, such as walnut or dark oak. Wipe on an even coat of stain, using a brush or clean cloth. Let the stain penetrate the wood for about one minute, and then wipe off the excess with a clean, dry cloth. Let the stain dry for at least four hours.

4 Apply furniture wax to the areas you want to distress, such as the edges and under any handles. Draw a quick sketch of the piece and mark the areas where you have applied the wax.

(continued next page)

5 Apply the lighter paint color over one side of the piece, painting with the grain of the wood. (Paint only one side at a time, because the paint must be wet for the next step.)

6 Working quickly, apply the darker paint color to the same side of the piece, blending the darker paint into the lighter shade. Continue painting one side at a time until the whole piece is painted. Let the paint dry at least 40 minutes, but no longer than an hour.

7 Scrape the paint off the areas where you applied furniture wax, using a putty knife. (If you don't remember exactly where you applied the wax, refer to the diagram you made in Step 4.)

8 Use fine-grit sandpaper to smooth any rough spots created by the putty knife. Let the piece dry completely.

9 Spray a coat of polyurethane finish on the entire piece and let it dry. Apply a second coat and let it dry.

10 When the finish is completely dry, replace the hardware.

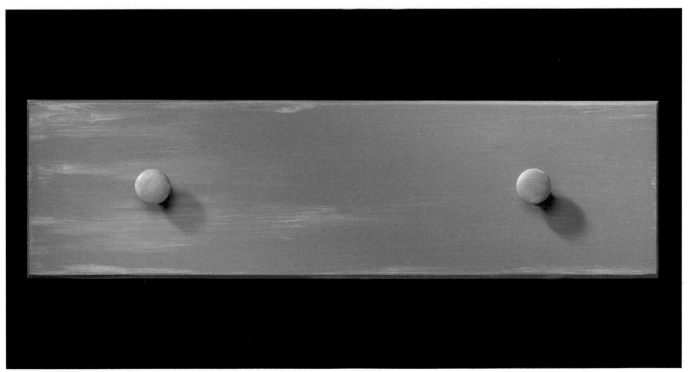

Variation: If you want paint rather than stain to show in the distressed areas, paint the entire piece and let it dry. Next, apply furniture wax to selected areas and then add the two paint colors and let them dry. Sand away the paint over the waxed areas, being careful to sand only down to the first paint color.

Aged Rubbed Finish

A rubbed finish is an easy and effective finish, especially on light wood, such as pine or white fir. It isn't necessary to distress a rubbed finish, but it does lend a little more character to the piece.

When distressing a rubbed finish, remember that the paint should be thoroughly dry. If possible, let the piece dry overnight before you start distressing it. Also, remember that the more you sand, the more worn the piece will appear. It's easy to go back and sand more but very difficult to successfully add paint, so work slowly and evaluate your work periodically.

TOOLS & MATERIALS

- Cordless screwdriver
- Medium-grit sandpaper
- Tack cloth
- Painter's tape (optional)
- Thick white cotton rag
- Flat, interior latex paint
- Satin-finish polyurethane spray

How to Create an Aged, Rubbed Finish

1 Tape brown paper over any glass and remove any hardware from the piece. If there are drawers, remove them. Lightly sand the surfaces, and then remove the sanding dust, using tack cloth.

2 Dip a thick cotton rag (a cloth diaper works great) into the paint. Using a back-and-forth motion and following the grain of the paint, rub the paint into the wood. Let the piece dry overnight.

3 Sand away some of the rubbed-on paint to reveal the wood beneath. Concentrate on areas where wear would naturally show—at corners, behind handles, and on the edges.

4 Wipe the entire piece with tack cloth to remove the paint residue. When the entire piece is clean, apply a light coat of clear polyurethane finish. Let the polyurethane dry, and then add a second coat. Remove the masking tape and paper, and set the piece aside to dry overnight. When the piece is thoroughly dry, replace the hardware.

Pickled Paint

*P*ickling is a simple effect created by painting the piece with watered-down paint and then removing the excess. The most important thing to remember when using this technique is to work quickly—the paint must still be wet as you wipe it away.

Pieces made of pine are good choices for this technique. Because it's very porous, pine absorbs the paint quickly, and plenty of color is left after the excess has been wiped away. Other softwoods will also work, but pieces made of hardwoods, such as oak, aren't good candidates for a pickled finish.

TOOLS & MATERIALS
- Cordless screwdriver
- Fine-grit sandpaper
- Tack cloth
- 2" small natural sponge
- Thick white cotton rag
- Flat-finish interior latex paint
- One quart of water
- Satin-finish polyurethane spray

How to Create a Pickled Finish

1 Remove drawers from dressers and upholstered seats from chairs. If the piece has hardware, remove carefully remove it.

2 Combine one part of paint with three parts of water. Stir the mixture thoroughly.

3 Paint the paint-and-water mixture onto the piece, using a small sponge. Follow the grain of the wood as you paint, and try to avoid drips and runs. If the piece is large, divide it into sections and complete one section before painting another.

4 Using a thick cotton rag, wipe excess paint off the piece. Work quickly, because the paint must be wet in order to be successfully removed.

(continued next page)

How to Create a Pickled Finish (continued)

5 Spray on a light coat of polyurethane finish and let it dry for an hour. Apply a second coat and let the piece dry overnight.

6 Replace the upholstered seat or hardware.

Replacing an Old Fabric Seat Cushion

1 If desired, change the fabric on the seat before replacing it. Pry up the staples and remove the old fabric. Use the old fabric as a pattern to cut a new piece.

2 Place the fabric upside down on a worktable. Wrap the fabric to the back of the seat and tape it in place. Turn the seat over and check the positioning of the fabric; adjust as necessary. Turn the seat back over and staple the fabric to the seat, placing a staple about every inch along the perimeter of the seat.

Variation

For pieces made of hardwoods or to create a more traditional look for a formal room, you can achieve a pickled effect with stain rather than paint. Select a water-based stain in a color of your choice.

Prepare the piece by removing any hardware and sanding the surface lightly (see page 267). Combine one part of stain with three parts of water and stir thoroughly.

Use a small sponge brush to apply the stain-water mixture, following the grain of the wood. While the mixture is still wet, wipe away any excess. Allow the piece to dry, then apply two coats of polyurethane spray (see pages 267 to 268). When the polyurethane is dry, replace the hardware as necessary.

Colorwash Technique

Colorwashing is another simple way to produce an interesting, somewhat uneven, finish. This is an easy technique, but it takes a little more time than some other finishes because it requires a coat of primer, two coats of a base color, and a final coat of wash. Each coat must dry before you move to the next step, so allow plenty of time for colorwash projects.

Although you can use a sponge or a rag to apply the glaze, bristle brushes create a nice sheer coat of glaze with good contrast between it and the base coat. Experiment with the glaze in an inconspicuous area before applying it to the whole project. You may want to apply the glaze in a circular motion or against the grain of the wood rather than with the grain as usual, but you really won't know what works best for the project until you try it.

If the glaze dries before you have thoroughly brushed it out, the finish will be uneven. Adding paint extender extends the drying time of the glaze and gives you more time to work with it.

TOOLS & MATERIALS

- Fine-grit sandpaper
- Tack cloth
- 2" sponge brush
- 1½" synthetic-bristle brush
- Latex primer
- Latex paint for base coat
- Latex paint for glaze coat
- Water-based glaze
- Paint extender
- Satin-finish polyurethane spray

How to Create a Colorwash Finish

1 Remove any drawers or hardware on the piece, and tape off any glass. Lightly sand the surfaces and remove the sanding dust with tack cloth.

2 Apply one coat of water-based primer, using a small sponge brush. Let the primer dry overnight, or according to the manufacturer's directions.

3 Apply a coat of the base color, using a 2" sponge brush. When the first coat is dry, apply a second, and let it dry.

4 Combine one part of the paint wash color with five parts glaze, and mix thoroughly. Brush the glaze onto the cabinet, and let it dry overnight.

(continued next page)

5 Spray a light coat of polyurethane finish onto the piece and let it dry. Apply a second coat and let it dry. Remove any masking tape, and replace any hardware or drawers.

TIP: You can use oil-based paint for this project as long as you use an oil-based primer and glaze.

Colorwash Variations

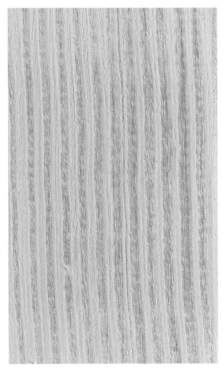

A dark wash over a light base will cause the woodwork to "recede" slightly in the room design.

A light wash over a dark base will brighten and highlight woodwork or furniture.

A vibrant color over a medium base creates a dramatic effect.

Crackled Finish

*I*t usually takes years, maybe even generations, for layers of paint to crack and peel. For people who enjoy the look of a crackled finish but don't want to wait years for the cracks to develop, a special, easy-to-use medium provides an almost instant solution.

Crackle medium is water based and works only with latex paints and glazes. Never use oil-based paints or glazes with crackle medium—like oil and water, they simply do not mix.

The crackled effect is enhanced by contrast between the base coat and top coat. You can further age the finish with a coat of tinted furniture wax if desired.

Only water-based paints and glazes are compatible with crackle medium. Tinted furniture wax enhances the illusion of age.

TOOLS & MATERIALS

- Fine-grit sanding sponge
- Small synthetic-bristle brush
- Two colors of flat, interior latex paint
- Crackling medium
- Tinted furniture wax

How to Create a Crackled Finish

1 Remove any drawers or doors and hardware. Lightly sand the surfaces, using a sanding sponge. (An absolutely smooth finish is not necessary for this technique, so light sanding is sufficient.) Wipe away the sanding residue with tack cloth.

2 Apply the base coat, following the grain of the wood. Let the paint dry completely.

3 Brush on the crackle medium. (Take care not to overbrush the medium, which would disrupt the crackling effect.) Allow the medium to dry according to manufacturer's directions.

4 Brush on the top coat of paint. Cracks will appear as the paint dries—be careful not to brush into areas that are already developing cracks. When the piece is painted, let it dry completely.

274 Advanced Painting & Decorating

Variation: Rub tinted furniture wax over the surface of the piece. (The wax will darken the space between the cracks and add an antique patina to the finish.)

Variation: Instead of using paint for the base coat, apply a water-based stain over the wood. When the stain dries, brush on the crackle medium and top coat as described.

Crackled Finish Variations

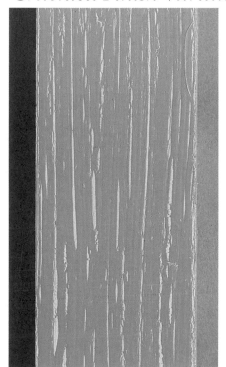

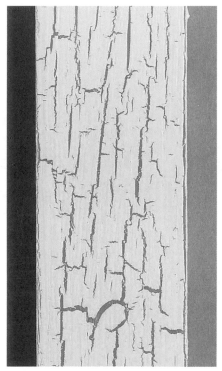

A dark top coat over a light base makes a strong decor statement.

A light top coat over a dark base creates a classic farmhouse look.

A vibrant color over a medium base works well to draw attention to a piece.

Lacquered Finish

*T*he secret to a perfect lacquered finish is deep, rich color and a smooth surface. Tinted primer helps produce deep colors, and extensive sanding results in a flawless surface.

Sanding may be, in fact, the most important part of the process. The high gloss of a lacquered finish highlights every surface flaw, even small ones, so meticulous sanding is essential.

Power sanders simplify the process of creating the flawless finish necessary for a successful lacquered finish.

TOOLS & MATERIALS

- Extra-fine-grit and fine-grit sandpaper
- Tack cloth
- 2" sponge brush
- Latex primer tinted to match the paint (deep colors only)
- Semigloss latex paint
- Gloss-finish polyurethane spray

How to Create a Lacquered Finish

1 Sand the piece thoroughly, using fine-grit sandpaper. Switch to the extra-fine-grit paper and sand again. Wipe away the sanding dust with tack cloth. Shine a bright light sideways over the piece, and check carefully for lumps or bumps. Run your hands lightly over the surface to check for flaws. Continue to sand until the surface is completely smooth.

2 Apply the first coat of primer and let it dry overnight. Lightly sand the surface, using an extra-fine grit sanding sponge. Wipe the piece down with tack cloth, and apply a second coat of primer. Let the primer dry overnight.

3 Brush the first coat of paint onto the piece, and let it dry. Sand the piece, again using the extra-fine sanding sponge and wiping away the residue with tack cloth. Apply a second coat of paint and let it dry.

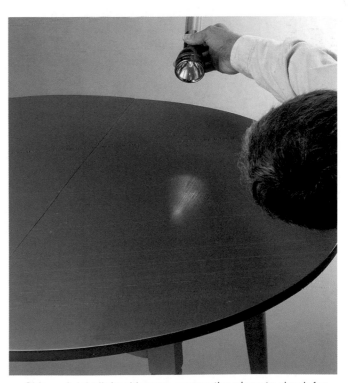

4 Shine a bright light sideways across the piece to check for surface flaws. If necessary, sand again. When the surface is completely smooth, apply two coats of gloss-finish polyurethane spray.

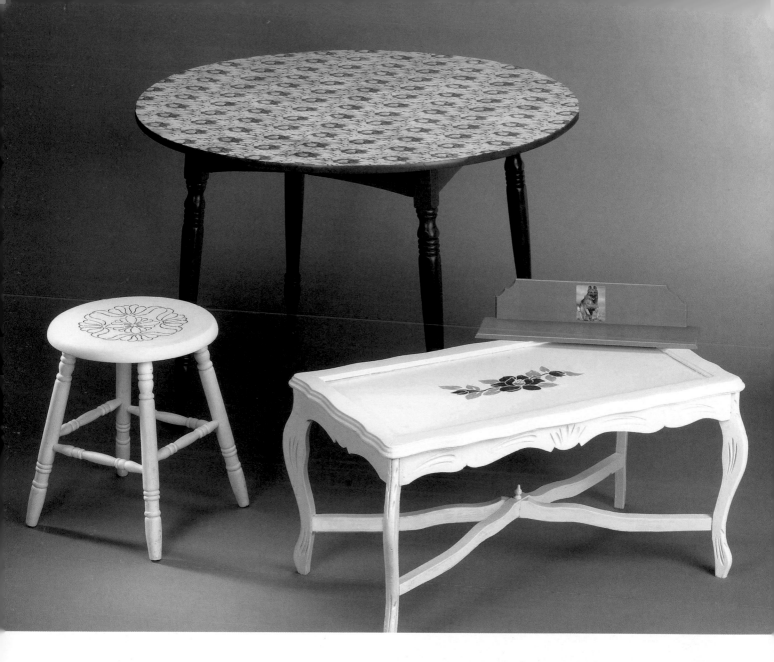

Special Effects

Everyday household items can be adapted for use in special painting projects. Color photocopies can be used for decoupage projects, inexpensive lace fabric can be used as a painting mask, and stencils—including quilting stencils—can be used to decorate otherwise plain pieces.

Once you've developed a repertoire of basic furniture painting skills, you'll be ready to branch out into special effects. In the following pages, we'll introduce you to several additional techniques for decorating painted furniture.

These simple techniques add texture, character, or personality to your projects. The best thing about these ideas is that you can easily adapt them to your own tastes and color schemes.

How to Paint Stripes

1 Sand the piece thoroughly and remove the sanding dust with tack cloth. Apply two coats of primer, letting it dry between coats. Apply two coats of the base color, letting it dry between coats. When the final coat is completely dry, measure the piece and plan the stripe pattern. Mask off the borders of the stripes, pressing the edges of the tape to seal it well.

2 Add the second color of paint, using a small paintbrush or sponge roller. Carefully remove the masking tape and let the piece dry.

How to Add Decoupage to a Painted Piece

1 Find a picture you want to use—it can be something from a calendar, a book, or even a color photocopy. Cut out the picture, following the design lines carefully. Apply decoupage medium to the design area and carefully position the picture.

2 Apply a coat of decoupage medium over the entire area and let it dry. Apply additional coats of medium, allowing it to dry completely between coats, until the surface of the picture has blended into the surface of the wood. Spray the entire piece with satin-finish polyurethane.

How to Add a Stencil to a Painted Piece

1 Paint the piece as desired, but do not apply the polyurethane finish. Position the stencil on the dry piece, and tape it in place. Dip a stencil brush into craft paint and blot off the excess paint on clean paper towels. Pounce the brush against the stencil, slowly filling it in with paint. Allow the first color to dry completely.

2 Continue adding one portion of the stencil at a time, until the design is complete. (Be sure to let the paint dry between stencils.) Apply two coats of satin-finish polyurethane spray.

How to Decorate a Piece Using a Quilt Stencil

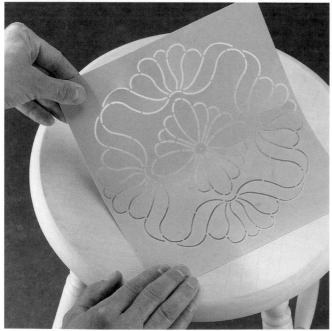

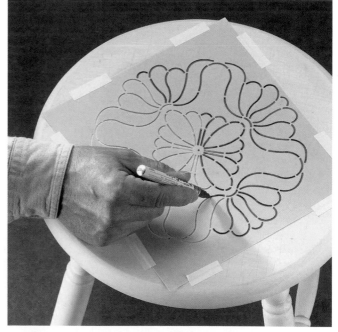

1 Paint the piece as desired, but do not apply the polyurethane finish. When the paint is completely dry, position a quilting stencil over the surface and tape it in place.

2 Trace inside each cut of the stencil, using a paint pen. If the piece is a dark color, try using a white or off-white paint pen; if it's light, use black or dark brown.

How to Create a Lacquered Finish

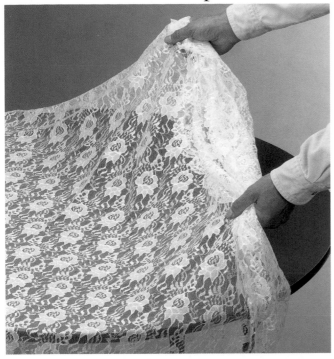

1 Paint the piece as desired, but do not apply the polyurethane. (The base color should be the color you want the "lace" to be—the background color will be added in the painting process.) Lay out the lace and determine where and how to position it for maximum effect.

2 Tape the lace in position. Make sure the lace is tight against the surface and be sure to smooth it out as carefully as possible—wrinkles could interrupt the design.

3 Evenly and lightly spray a coat of paint over the lace, holding the paint can about 10 inches from the surface. Try to avoid touching or bumping the lace. Let the paint dry for an hour, then remove the tape. Carefully lift the lace straight up from the surface so you don't disturb the paint.

4 When the paint is completely dry, apply two coats of satin-finish polyurethane spray to the entire piece. Let the finish dry between coats.

Converting Measurements

To Convert:	To:	Multiply by:
Inches	Millimeters	25.4
Inches	Centimeters	2.54
Feet	Meters	0.305
Yards	Meters	0.914
Square inches	Square centimeters	6.45
Square feet	Square meters	0.093
Square yards	Square meters	0.836
Cubic inches	Cubic centimeters	16.4
Cubic feet	Cubic meters	0.0283
Cubic yards	Cubic meters	0.765
Ounces	Millileters	30.0
Pints (U.S.)	Liters	0.473 (Imp. 0.568)
Quarts (U.S.)	Liters	0.946 (Imp. 1.136)
Gallons (U.S.)	Liters	3.785 (Imp. 4.546)
Ounces	Grams	28.4
Pounds	Kilograms	0.454

To Convert:	To:	Multiply by:
Millimeters	Inches	0.039
Centimeters	Inches	0.394
Meters	Feet	3.28
Meters	Yards	1.09
Square centimeters	Square inches	0.155
Square meters	Square feet	10.8
Square meters	Square yards	1.2
Cubic centimeters	Cubic inches	0.061
Cubic meters	Cubic feet	35.3
Cubic meters	Cubic yards	1.31
Millileters	Ounces	.033
Liters	Pints (U.S.)	2.114 (Imp. 1.76)
Liters	Quarts (U.S.)	1.057 (Imp. 0.88)
Liters	Gallons (U.S.)	0.264 (Imp. 0.22)
Grams	Ounces	0.035
Kilograms	Pounds	2.2

Liquid Measurement Equivalents

1 Tablespoon		= 3 Teaspoons
1 Fluid Ounce		= 2 Tablespoons
1 Cup	= 8 Fluid Ounces	= 16 Tablespoons
1 Pint	= 16 Fluid Ounces	= 2 Cups
1 Quart	= 32 Fluid Ounces	= 2 Pints
1 Gallon	= 128 Fluid Ounces	= 4 Quarts

Calculating Room Dimensions

Wall height	= Distance from floor to ceiling
Wall length	= Distance from corner to corner
Square footage (area in feet)	
Wall	= Length × Height
Floor	= Length × Width
Ceiling	= Length × Width
Perimeter	= Length of all walls

Converting Temperatures

Convert degrees Fahrenheit (F) to degrees Celsius (C) by following this simple formula: Subtract 32 from the Fahrenheit temperature reading. Then, mulitply that number by 5⁄9. For example, 77°F - 32 = 45. 45 × 5⁄9 = 25°C.

To convert degrees Celsius to degrees Fahrenheit, multiply the Celsius temperature reading by 9⁄5. Then, add 32. For example, 25°C × 9⁄5 = 45. 45 + 32 = 77°F.

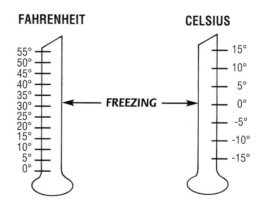

Abrasive Paper Grits - (Aluminum Oxide)

VERY COARSE	COARSE	MEDIUM	FINE	VERY FINE
12 - 36	40 - 60	80 - 120	150 - 180	220 - 600

Index

Resources

The following manufacturers contributed photography and information for this book. For more information on their products, contact them at the addresses below.

Anaglypta/Lincrusta
Crown House
Darwen, Lancashire, England
tel: (44) 254-704-951
fax: (44) 254-760-700
www.anaglypta.com

Blonder Wallcoverings
3950 Prospect Avenue
Cleveland, OH 44115
tel: 216-431-3560
fax: 216-431-5367
www.blonderwall.com

Modern Masters, Inc.
13201 Saticoy St.
N. Hollywood, CA 91605
tel: 800-942-3166
fax: 818-765-2915
www.modernmastersinc.com

ORAC DECOR by Outwater Plastics Industries, Inc.
Architectural Division
22 Passaic Street
Wood-Ridge, NJ 07075
tel: 800-631-8375
fax: 800-888-3315
www.outwater.com

Photot Credits

p. 11: ©Naill McDiarmid/Alamy.

p. 13: © Tony Giammarino for designer Robert Rentz.

p. 15: © Digistock/Alamy.

p. 17: © Tony Giammarino.

p. 19: © Digistock/Alamy.

p. 21: © Andrea Rugg for Trehus Builders, Minneapolis, MN and Meriwether Felt Architects, Denver, CO.

pp. 22-23: © Photodisc/Getty Images, Inc.

p. 25: (left) © Tony Giammarino; (right) © Photodisc/Getty Images, Inc.

p. 26: © Andrea Rugg for Otogawa-Anschel Design & Build.

p. 27: © Elizabeth Whiting and Associates/Alamy.

p. 28: © Mode Images Limited/Alamy.

p. 29: (left) © Digistock/Alamy; (right) © Brand X Pictures.

pp. 30-31: © Tony Giammarino for designer Beth Sheer.

p. 33: (left): Photo courtesy of Blonder Wallcoverings; (right) © Elizabeth Whiting and Associates/Alamy.

p. 34: © Brand X Pictures.

p. 35: © Tony Giammarino.

p. 36: © Ivan Bárta/Alamy.

p. 37: (left) Photo courtesy of Blonder Wallcoverings; (right) © Elizabeth Whiting and Associates/ Alamy.

p. 38: © Tony Giammarino for designer/painter Patti Ryan.

p. 39: (left) Photo Courtesy of Modern Masters ®; (right) © Brand X Pictures.

p. 42: (top) © Tony Giammarino for designer/painter Patti Ryan.

p. 43: (top) © Tony Giammarino.

p. 44: © Tony Giammarino for designer/painter Patti Ryan.

p. 45: © Tony Giammarino for designer Christine McCabe.

p. 46: © Tony Giammarino for designer Beth Sheer.

p. 47: © Digistock/Alamy.

pp. 48-49: © Elizabeth Whiting and Associates/Alamy.

pp. 192-193: (all) © Quarto Publishing Plc.

pp. 200-206: (all) © Quarto Publishing Plc.

pp. 210-211: (all) © Quarto Publishing Plc.

p. 212: © Tony Giammarino for designer Beth Sheer.

p. 238: (top) © Tony Giammarino.

p. 244: Photo courtesy of Analypta/Lincrusta.

p. 247: Photo courtesy of Analypta/Lincrusta.

pp. 252-253: Photos courtesy of ORAC DECOR by Outwater Plastics Industries, Inc.

p. 255: (bottom left, center and right) Photos courtesy of ORAC DECOR by Outwater Plastics Industries, Inc.

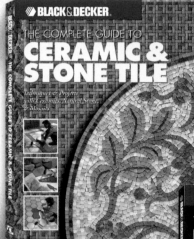